JB JOSSEY-BASS™
A Wiley Brand

T0314157

How to Communicate More Effectively with Donors, Members & Volunteers

Scott C. Stevenson, Editor

WILEY

978-1-118-69310-0   ISBN

978-1-118-70436-3   ISBN (online)

How to Communicate More Effectively With Donors, Members & Volunteers

Published by

Stevenson, Inc.

P.O. Box 4528 • Sioux City, Iowa • 51104
Phone 712.239.3010 • Fax 712.239.2166
www.stevensoninc.com

TABLE OF CONTENTS

Article Designation Key: Donors ▪▪▪   Members ▪▪▪   Volunteers ▪▪▪

TABLE OF CONTENTS

1 Send Would-be Donors The Right Message

Most donors prefer to give to a winning organization rather than one that is struggling. As you meet with prospects and make your case:

- Do offer compelling reasons to invest in your cause; don't paint a picture of despair.

- Do provide a candid look at the challenges facing your organization, but also share the ways in which you are already addressing them.

- Do point out the benefits of investing in your charity, but don't make your organization's future contingent upon a donor's gift.

- Do be genuine in your delivery, but don't underestimate the power of enthusiasm in compelling others to give.

3 Use Postcards to Realize Direct Marketing Success

Sending a postcard is a fast, efficient and — at just 44 cents plus printing costs — inexpensive way to communicate with your membership. Whether you're announcing an event or sending details about a fundraiser, follow these tips for clear, clean communication:

1. Use an unusually colored or textured paper stock so your mailer won't get lost among other mail.

3. Use a bold, decisive headline and eye-catching images to draw in the member to read your mail piece.

4. Make your message clear and concise. Relay one message per mailer.

5. Ask for a response. Whether you're inviting members to an event or enticing more to join, be sure to ask for a response by a specific deadline.

6. With the easy use of current software programs, creative staffers can easily design effective postcards to reach your members.

7. For the best response, follow up, contacting members by phone or with a follow-up mailer before the deadline.

8. Track responses. When following up with members by phone, ask if they remember receiving the postcard and track how many respond by the deadline from the initial mailing.

2 Retain Members With Key Sections in Newsletter ■

Whether you offer a paper or online newsletter, consider adding the following sections to better serve your members and facilitate member retention:

✓ **Membership benefit highlights:** Single out lesser-known benefits available to members. Feature how active members are using the benefits and gaining from them.

✓ **Volunteer activities:** Highlight these to help members be active and serve your cause.

✓ **Member features:** Give readers a peek at the lives of members and feature their efforts within your organization. Share how a member became president or an officer to inform and inspire readers who may be interested in a higher role in the organization.

✓ **Member anniversaries:** If you provide a gift to members at five or 10 years of membership, write about this in the newsletter.

✓ **Membership numbers:** Encourage readers to find the current membership number in the publication and enter online for a prize. List winners in the next newsletter.

4 Boost Efficiency With Double-duty Brown-bag Meetings ■ ■ ■

Successful time management is crucial to achieving daily goals. By offering a lunchtime meeting, you may just accomplish all your tasks for the day.

Set up a policy where every Friday, staff and members are invited to join you for an informal bring-your-own-lunch meeting that includes a weekly recap.

This simple approach to conducting meetings allows participants to complete two tasks in one sitting, shaving an hour off the day. Don't go overboard by suggesting such a meeting every day or your staff could start feeling chained to their work.

Before implementing brown-bag meetings, ask staff and members to contribute their ideas for successful lunch meetings. Getting their buy-in helps ensure success.

5 Write One Note Each Day ■ ■ ■

Writing one note every morning — either to a donor, volunteer, board member, etc. — is an excellent way to maintain a multitude of important contacts. The handwritten note is one of the most personal forms of communication. Regardless of content, it establishes a personal rapport with the recipient.

6 Sharpen Your Communications Skills ▪▪ ▪▪ ▪▪

Whether speaking with members, staff or colleagues, communicating effectively is paramount to getting results. These simple guidelines will help you do so:

✓ **Listen with an open mind.** See every new conversation as a clean slate. Listen and focus on the conversation without interrupting the speaker. Summarize your interpretation of what you've been told to be sure you understood what you heard.

✓ **Drop your defenses.** Assume everyone is working with good intentions and that there is no ulterior motive to a request or comment. Don't let a bad morning, for example, influence how you listen and respond to this afternoon's conversation.

✓ **Ask open-ended questions.** When talking with a member who is expressing a concern, respond with open-end-ed questions that lead to more details. Avoid questions that result in only a "yes" or "no" answer or you may not get all the facts.

✓ **Take a positive approach.** Listen intently without allowing yourself to become distracted. Thank the person for the information and suggest the next plan of action.

✓ **Be mindful of body language.** Slouching, turning away or folding your arms on your chest can relay disinterest or disagreement. Watch the body language of others involved in the conversation to determine if they are giving you their full attention.

✓ **Lead by example.** Actions speak louder than words. Want your staff to be attentive and action-focused? Project the behavior you would like them to project.

7 Ask Your CEO to Thank First-time Contributors ▪▪

Nonprofits with a history of fundraising generally have a well-thought-out gift acknowledgment procedure in place. But whether you're new at fundraising or well established, it makes sense to treat first-time contributors with kid gloves. To build a habit of giving, they deserve some special attention.

That's why it makes sense to have your executive director or president send first-time contributors a note of appreciation after that gift arrives.

If you have hundreds of first-time givers annually, you will want to simplify the gift acknowledgment process. If, on the other hand, first-time contributors amount to only a handful of sources, a personal handwritten note makes most sense. In either instance, however, getting a personal message from the CEO makes an impact that's worth doing.

If your organization receives lots of first-time gifts, you may choose to develop a simplified thank-you note that your CEO can simply sign and, when time permits, add a more personal P.S. such as the example shown here.

> February 4, 2009
>
> Dear Scott and Susan,
>
> When I was told you had made a gift to our museum, I wanted to extend my heartfelt thanks and welcome you to our family of supporters.
>
> Gifts such as yours, regardless of size, allow us to do so much more than we otherwise would be able to accomplish.
>
> Sometime in the near future you will receive an invitation to attend one of our quarterly members-only receptions. I hope you can attend so I can thank you in person.
>
> Sincerely,
>
> *Bill*
>
> Bill Thompson
> Executive Director
>
> *P.S. I also just learned you are new parents. Congratulations!*

8 Know in Advance What You Plan to Say ▪▪

When planning to set an appointment with a prospect, know what you plan to say before picking up the phone.

Before attempting to make a new contact, write a brief script you can review prior to calling for an appointment. It should introduce who you represent and give a compelling reason why a face-to-face meeting would be mutually beneficial. Always keep the prospect's interests foremost, and ask for the appointment early in the conversation.

As you formulate the reason for a meeting, keep the "so what" factor in mind. Imagine the prospect responding by saying "so what" after each reason you offer. Doing that will allow you to view the justification for an appointment through the eyes of the person you hope to see.

9 ## Develop a Brochure Template That You Can Customize ■ ■■ ■■

Need a simple but cost-effective way to promote various involvement opportunities?

Develop a brochure template that can be used to create any number of brochures describing your organization's different volunteer projects. Having a standard template with standard categories in hand means that you need only fill in the blanks to produce any number of in-house brochures to hand out, stuff in envelopes or otherwise target groups of would-be volunteers.

As an example, use a standard 8 1/2 X 11-inch sheet to create a folded three-panel brochure (many computer programs come with such templates already created and ready for your modification). Folded, the front panel would include your agency's name, optional logo or line art and name of the particular project you're promoting. Unfolded, the inside would describe the program in detail, with the third panel used as a tear-off return form with your mailing address on one side and information to be completed by the volunteer on the other, so the volunteer need only tear it off, fill it out, add a stamp and drop it in the mail to you.

Some information in the brochure would remain the same regardless of the project/program being described, while other information would be tailored to that particular project/program, giving all your brochures a similar look people will come to identify with your organization.

To add two-color flair to your brochures, have preprints made in colored ink (on a paper style and weight of your choice) featuring information that will be identical regardless of brochure content (e.g., your organization's name, logo/line art and return address). When you need a brochure for a specific project, create the text unique to that program, format it to fit on the preprint, then run the brochure off on a copier, so the project-specific information is added in black.

[You may choose to put your organization's logo or line art illustration here]

The Howard County Museum
Alpine, Vermont

Get Involved —
Join Our Speaker's Bureau

Left: Sample front panel of tri-fold, 8 1/2 X 11-inch brochure template.

Below: Two inside panels — some content is same on all brochures and some tailored to the volunteer project you're promoting.

The Howard County Museum
Speaker's Bureau Program —
[Description of speaker's bureau program]

How It Works —
[Description of what speakers bureau volunteers do]

Volunteer Qualifications —
[Description of volunteer qualifications]

The Howard County Museum
Speaker's Bureau Program —

Interested? Want more information about how it works? Simply complete this form, return it to us and we'll be in touch. It's that simple!

❑ *I'd like to know more. Please contact me.*
❑ *I'm definitely interested. Sign me up!*

Name_____
Address _____
City/State/ZIP _____
Daytime Phone _____
E-mail _____

10 Enhance Member Benefits With Teleseminars ■■

Teleseminars are an easy, cost-effective way to provide information to your members.

Schedule a monthly or bi-monthly teleseminar that can be recorded and played back at your member's convenience.

Use external experts or member experts to talk about subjects that will help your members grow their business. You can use a question-and-answer format or allow the speaker to discuss the topic for approximately 40 to 45 minutes and leave the rest of the time open for questions.

Often outside speakers will provide their expertise at no charge in exchange for the free publicity and/or a copy of the teleseminar that they can resell to their other clients.

Your members simply dial a number and press a code to connect to the conference. You can find services that are toll-free (more expensive for the association) or that are regular toll fees for your members. Many services provide the option of muting the guest's phone line so that the call is not interrupted with dogs barking or babies crying.

You can provide handouts that are downloaded at your website to add more benefit to the call. Place a link to download the teleseminar so that your members can listen to it on their Ipod or computer.

Follow Up Visits With a Summary Letter

Each face-to-face visit you have with a planned gift prospect is important. You will no doubt have some objective in mind each time you meet with a prospect — introduction, cultivation, solicitation or stewardship.

Following each visit, it's important to send a letter summarizing your meeting, especially since many aspects of planned gifts can be more technical and unique to the type of gift being considered, the gift amount, the age of the donor(s) and more.

A follow-up letter allows you to reiterate key discussion points and suggest next steps in formalizing a planned gift. Such a letter also helps to reflect a higher level of professionalism.

The generic letter shown here illustrates how a follow-up letter might read depending on the nature of your visit, what's being discussed and the unique characteristics of the individual with whom you are meeting.

**Stone's Throw
Academy**

Dear Frank:

As always, it was a pleasure to have met with you this past week. I always enjoy our visits and have such great respect for you.

I thought it might be helpful to summarize our conversation as you consider the benefits of establishing a charitable gift annuity for XYZ Nonprofit.

Based on your age of 70, you could establish a charitable gift annuity that pays an annuity rate of 6.5 percent. In exchange for a cash gift of $10,000, XYZ Nonprofit will provide you with an annuity of $650 per year for the remainder of your lifetime. Of that $650, $280.15 will be treated as ordinary income and the remaining $369.85 as tax-free income (until year 2021). In addition, you can claim a current federal charitable income tax deduction of $4,118.47.

Also as we discussed, instead of using cash to fund your gift annuity, you could fund it with appreciated stock and receive additional tax benefits. By funding the gift annuity with stock that has appreciated in value and that has been owned for longer than one year, you would significantly reduce the federal and state capital gains taxes that would have accrued had you sold the stock yourself.

I'm assuming you may have additional questions about this type of gift so I'll plan to get in touch in a couple of weeks to set another time for us to get together and chat more about it.

Thanks again, Frank, for meeting with me and weighing the benefits — to you and to XYZ Nonprofit — of establishing a charitable gift annuity.

Sincerely,

Robert Griffin
Planned Gifts Director

---

12   Tailor Presentations to Individuals' Interests ▬ ▬ ▬

Learning to tailor individual presentations to would-be donors' interests is a craft that requires thorough prospect research and sensitive listening skills. That's why knowing as much as possible about a prospects' interests prior to the solicitation is so important.

Sometimes prospects' interests will have a direct link to funding projects while at other times the relationship will be more abstract.

Whether through cultivation visits prior to solicitation or other research efforts, work to garner information to help identify your prospects' interests and shape your solicitation. Below are categories to help you learn more about prospects.

Interest Categories, Key Facts

Here are some interest categories and important information that may be helpful to know about your major gift prospects:

Personal Interests
- Importance placed on family
- Leisure-time activities
- What matters most in life
- Importance placed on education
- Financial philosophy
- Philanthropic interests
- Civic involvement/interests
- Future hopes and plans
- Close friends
- Pet peeves
- Personal heroes
- Religious preference/importance

Political Persuasion
- Conservative versus liberal
- Passive versus strong opinions
- Opinions on social issues

Business/Career
- Career progression
- Current responsibilities
- Accomplishments and setbacks
- Business connections
- Management style
- Community, statewide and national involvement

---

13   Use E-newsletters to Increase Participation ▬ ▬ ▬

An effective, regular e-newsletter can increase membership participation.

The Families of Spinal Muscular Atrophy (SMA) of Libertyville, IL began sending a monthly e-newsletter, Connections, to its 5,000 members a year ago, says Lenna Scott, communications director.

Since then, the increase in member feedback has given the organization ideas to improve services and benefits, says Scott. More members also are participating in fundraising efforts through the newsletter.

The key to this success is to include easy ways for members to communicate with the organization in the newsletter by providing links and e-mails they can click on to read and send messages.

"We've seen an increase in fundraising, because all members have to do is click on a link to participate," says Scott. "For nonprofits, keeping fundraisers that simple is critical."

Following are steps for starting your organization's e-newsletter:

1. **Update your e-mail database.** Collect member's e-mail addresses on registration forms, at conferences and member events.

2. **Determine your goals.** Scott says the organization chose a Web-based software program, Constant Contact, to achieve its goal of improving the quality of e-mails sent to members. The program also tracks e-mails that have been opened and forwarded; it updates the subscriber database, saving staff time and money.

3. **Plan the information you want sent to members.** Connections includes a balance of scientific updates, events, fundraising and legislative news. Issues also regularly profile a member family or a special event.

4. **Be responsive to your membership.** After the e-newsletter is published, use feedback to gauge what to continue and discontinue in the publication.

Source: Lenna Scott, Communications Director, Families of Spinal Muscular Atrophy, Libertyville, IL. Phone (800) 886-1762. E-mail: lenna@fsma.org

14 Reflection Sessions Identify What's Working, What's Not ▪

Do you make a point to regularly seek input from your volunteers? After all, they're the ones on the front line and probably know best what's working and what's not.

Make a point to conduct informal reflection sessions from time to time. At the end of their work period, meet with them for some casual questions and answers that seek their opinions of the task at hand. Besides focusing on their work, ask questions about them — what they like and dislike about the project; what energizes them and keeps them coming back; and so forth.

Evaluating programs and volunteer experiences need not always be a formal process. You can gain great insight into volunteers' experiences through a simple, half-hour reflection session.

15 Share Both Ups and Downs With Your Members ▪ ▪ ▪

Don't just share the good news in member publications. Detail your challenges as well.

At the end of each quarter or year, include a recap in your written or online newsletter that details the positive highlights as well as some of the challenges your organization has faced. Obviously, you do not want to share anything that would unnecessarily alarm your members. However, sharing some of your minor disappointments will give members insight into what your goals are and how you accomplish them.

For example, if you had planned to grow your membership by 25 percent but did not meet that goal, explain what you plan to do in the coming months to achieve this goal. Along with each challenge or disappointment you list, include how you dealt with the situation or what you are working on to handle the situation in a new way.

Disclosing highs and lows will create a better flow of communication between your staff and those you serve, and could even generate fresh ideas for solutions from members.

16 Communication Key to Building Donor Relationships ▪

How do you build a habit of giving among first-time donors? Communication.

"Communication about the success of your programs is key to motivating people to give," says Valerie Ingram, development director, Santa Fe Community Foundation (Santa Fe, NM). "If donors can connect a benefit to a real person that was made possible with their gift, they know their investment ... was well placed. If they trust that the organization is using donations effectively, they will give again."

Carrie Hoppe, executive director, the University of Wisconsin-Sheboygan Foundation (Sheboygan, WI), agrees.

"Giving is not something that always comes naturally for some donors," says Hoppe. "You must build trust and credibility, and regular communication can do that. You must remain in contact with new donors and build a connection between them and your institution or organization in order for them to feel comfortable adding your project or campaign to their philanthropic endeavor schedule."

Accomplish this habit of giving and your organization will certainly benefit.

If donors are not aware of donation requests in a timely manner, they may not have the funds available, Hoppe says. "But if that gift becomes part of an annual budget, it is much more likely that a nonprofit will see a donation and possibly a larger donation."

Additionally, Ingram says, "retention of longtime supporters is less expensive than acquiring new donors, both in terms of cost and time. If someone is in the habit of giving to your organization, all they need to continue to give is thanks and good communication about what your organization accomplishes."

Sources: Valerie Ingram, Development Director, Santa Fe Community Foundation, Santa Fe, NM. Phone (505) 988-9715. E-mail: vingram@santafecf.org
Carrie Hoppe, Executive Director, University of Wisconsin-Sheboygan Foundation, Sheboygan, WI. Phone (920) 459-6654. E-mail: carrie.hoppe@uwc.edu

17 Express Appreciation With a Letter to the Editor ▪ ▪ ▪

Marc Jordan, president & CEO, United Way of Central Virginia (Lynchburg, VA), expressed appreciation to more than 1,700 volunteers for their contribution to the annual Day of Caring by sending a letter to the editor. It is a simple way to publicly thank volunteers, while describing your mission and acknowledging sponsors.

Jordan's letter to the Lynchburg News and Advance focused on the community impact of the Day of Caring event. He also acknowledged major sponsors by name and asked readers to visit their facilities. Copies were sent to each sponsor, while volunteers could share their success with family and friends.

Source: R. Marc Jordan, President & CEO, United Way of Central Virginia, Lynchburg, VA. Phone (434) 455-6901. E-mail: marc.Jordan@unitedwaycv.org

President's Letter Creates Connection With Members ■

Including a personal letter from your president, CEO or board president in membership publications is a great way to establish personal connections with your members while also informing them of significant news.

Several years ago, staff with the Greater Oklahoma City Chamber (Oklahoma City, OK) began including Leadership Notes, a letter written by the chamber president, in their membership newsletter (see example, below).

The president, Roy Williams, created the feature as a way to introduce himself to the members, says Lisa Boevers, vice president, membership.

The letters touch on a variety of issues regarding community news, accomplishments and member campaigns, Boevers says. The goal of each letter, she says, "is for the president to connect with membership in a more personal way."

The feature allows the chamber staff to focus attention on key issues that the organization is working on, inform members of the chamber's stand on various issues and ask for help with a campaign when necessary, she says.

"If there is good news to share about our city or an accomplishment, it's the perfect place to share that information," says Boevers. "Newsletter articles are typically more fact-based news stories. A letter provides an opportunity for more editorial content."

When including a letter from the president in membership publications, she suggests placing it at the beginning of the publication so members will immediately notice it, and including the president's photo so members become more familiar with him/her.

Source: Lisa W. Boevers, Vice President, Membership, Greater Oklahoma City Chamber, Oklahoma City, OK. Phone (405) 297-8948

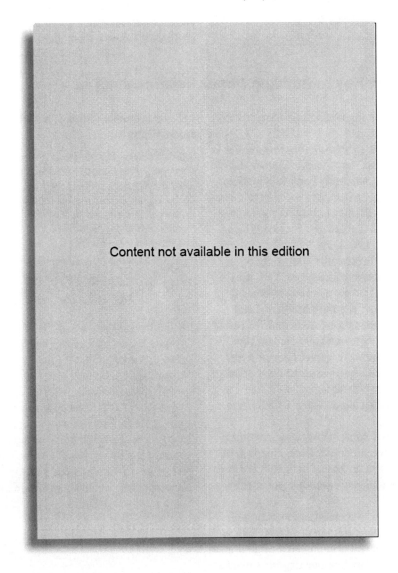

Content not available in this edition

19   Create a Website for Donors ▪

Instead of printing and mailing your donor report, why not make it available on your website?

St. Olaf College (Northfield, MN) chose to create the Partners Report, an annual fund magazine, instead of mailing a traditional donor report. "During our alumni focus groups we learned people wanted to read about how their dollars were benefiting current students," says Megan Astry, associate director of annual giving. "So we created the Partners Report with editorial pieces, pictures, charts and graphs to illustrate specific uses for annual fund donations. The printed piece looks like a magazine with stories and colorful layouts."

The actual list of its fiscal year donors was excluded from the magazine. "We wanted to be good stewards of our money," says Astry. "Instead of printing thousands of donor names in the Partners Report, we made an interactive website to serve as the donor list." To supplement the magazine, the college directed its constituents to their donor report website (www.stolaf.edu/donors) which contains a search engine for donor names and key pages from the Partners Report.

On the website, visitors can search for donors or classmates by name, class, giving category or donor type. Donors can also log into a special feature, using their alumni ID and password found on their magazine, to post why they give. When the donor shares why they give to the college, a visitor can click "view" after their name and the donor's submission appears. "We wanted to make the website interactive, so our donors would have a reason to visit the site and have a reason to come back," says Astry.

The website also features articles from the printed piece. This allows staff to track what is most often read and what types of information donors want to know. For example, staff knew donors were highly interested in how annual fund donations affected St. Olaf rankings in college guides because of the high number of click-throughs on that article. Using that information, staff can better target their future direct mail messages.

Source: Megan Astry, Associate Director of Annual Giving, St. Olaf College, Northfield, MN. Phone (507) 786-3705. E-mail: astry@stolaf.edu

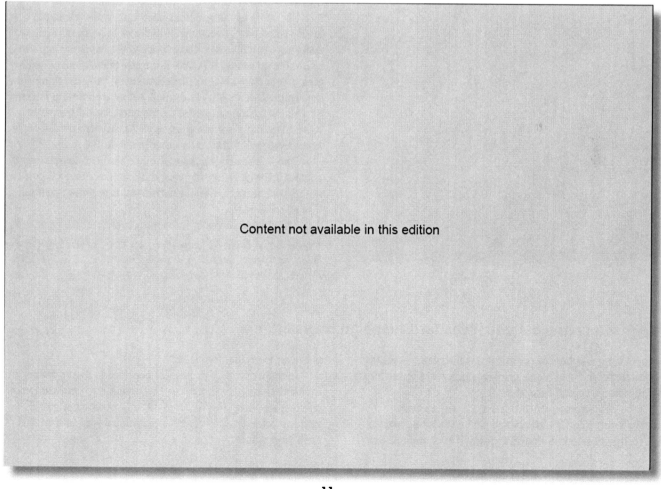

Content not available in this edition

Content not available in this edition

22 Targeted Website Helps Train, Recruit, Retain Volunteers

Your organization's website may be the first contact many potential volunteers have with your nonprofit. Make sure it is not their last by offering detailed information about your volunteer opportunities.

"I think it's important for volunteers to know exactly what the various positions entail before they sign on to assist," says Karen Neely Faryniak, associate vice president for college relations, Dickinson College (Carlisle, PA). "Otherwise, we're setting them and us up for failure."

To help website visitors understand what is involved with volunteering for the college, staff created the Dickinson Volunteer Network — a subsite dedicated solely to providing prospective and existing volunteers with timely, useful information.

Part of the college's general website, the site (www. dickinson.edu/volunteer/) entices visitors with the welcoming words: "Browse through the menu at the top of the page to learn why you should volunteer and what's new at Dickinson. The menu on the left will direct you to specific volunteer areas."

Clicks on those links lead visitors to full volunteer job descriptions for each opportunity, volunteer testimonials, ongoing training opportunities, contact information and video messages from President William G. Durden.

The site's job descriptions page is its website's fourth most-visited page, following only the main page, the admissions page and the page that lists all of the volunteer opportunities. Faryniak says this rank illustrates that alumni are taking their prospective volunteer roles seriously, fully checking out the responsibilities of the positions before committing to them.

Video training modules on the site serve as primary training tools for some volunteer roles, which Faryniak says saves time and money over other methods.

One adjustment made on the site has been to make staff contact information easily accessible up front, says Faryniak, noting that doing so alleviates frustration and the potential loss of a volunteer.

The college currently has approximately 2,500 volunteers.

Source: Karen Neely Faryniak, Associate Vice President for College Relations, Dickinson College, Carlisle, PA. Phone (717) 245-1578. E-mail: faryniak@dickinson.edu

23 Communications Ideas for Campaign Newsletter

Increasing numbers of organizations distribute a regular newsletter to constituents prior to, during and immediately following a capital campaign.

A campaign newsletter is a great way to keep people informed and motivated, and can also be used as a recognition tool. Some charities will even include the publication on their websites.

Include snapshot profiles of donors and their gifts in each campaign newsletter issue to give life to your campaign and inspire others to give. Equally important, spotlighting persons in the profiles offers an additional way to steward deserving donors.

24 At-a-glance Chart Shows Donors Where the Money Goes

Giving donors what they want and delivering on the services you promise are two keys to keeping donors happy. One thing donors want to know is that their gifts are making a difference. You can easily do that with a simple chart. Here's how:

1. Set aside one team meeting for brainstorming examples for the chart.

2. Put donation amounts down the left side and different programs along the top of chart.

3. Come up with specific examples of where a donor's money goes at that donation level in a certain program (e.g., an after-school mentoring center might spend $50 on craft supplies for summer camp, $100 on computer software for technology programs and $250 on one week's worth of snacks).

4. Copy the list and circulate to all staff for use in publications, conversations with constituents, speaking engagements, etc.

Having such examples at the ready is a simple way to give donors real details on what their money can do. Update the list to reflect cost increases and new opportunities.

25 Create a Members-only Column

Give your members a creative outlet by establishing a members-only column in your magazine or newsletter. Creating a section for members to share their history and experience is a great way to encourage readership and participation.

"The First Person Singular section in the association's monthly magazine is typically a 1,000- to 1,500-word article which reflects the experiences of any member or reader," says Andrew N. Vittoria, Jr., deputy executive director, Association of Old Crows (Alexandria, VA). "Alternatively, anyone with an appropriate story to tell can speak to a member of our editorial staff and we will be happy to wordsmith the article for the contributor to review before publication."

Creating a space in your publication for members to share stories creates camaraderie among your members and adds something unique to the publications you produce. "What we are looking for are stories recounting the personal experiences of current or former military personnel or civilians, where the role of electronic warfare technology or operations played a central part. Our readers enjoy reading it because it's: 1) written by fellow members; 2) something they can relate to; and 3) different than the other information in the magazine," says Vittoria.

Source: Andrew N. Vittoria, Jr., Deputy Executive Director, Association of Old Crows, Alexandria, VA. Phone (703) 549-1600.

26 Create a Volunteer Handbook That Serves Two Purposes

Celebrate and educate. That's what staff of the Chicago Department of Cultural Affairs (Chicago, IL) do through the organization's Summer Festival Volunteer Handbook.

"The handbook idea grew out of necessity as I realized I was repeating myself and the role volunteers play," says Marianne Wolf-Astrauskas, director of volunteers. "It made sense to use the handbook as an educational tool, but it made even more sense to use it to celebrate those who help us."

The 16-page handbook features:

- The organization's mission.
- Festival descriptions and facts.
- Volunteer opportunities.
- Contact information.
- Department policies.

Additionally, the handbook is full of color photographs featuring volunteers working at past festivals which, Wolf-Astrauskas says, speaks volumes.

When creating the handbook, she sought out photos of volunteers who contributed significant hours. Doing so, she says, helped show the volunteers and others that the Chicago Department of Cultural Affairs appreciated them.

The photos of volunteers on the job also show new volunteers what to expect, such as what festival booths look like and how to dress for the festival, she says. The photos also help put a face with a name as photos of on-site contacts are included.

In addition, text backs up each of the concepts shown in the photos.

"The feedback has been tremendous and positive," Wolf-Astrauskas says. "The volunteers have let us know how helpful and resourceful the handbook is."

Source: Marianne Wolf-Astrauskas, Director of Volunteers, Chicago Department of Cultural Affairs, Chicago, IL. Phone (312) 744-7096. E-mail: marianne.wolf@ cityofchicago.org

---

Draft a Training Handbook That Celebrates Volunteers

Marianne Wolf-Astrauskas, director of volunteers, Chicago Department of Cultural Affairs (Chicago, IL), offers the following suggestions for organizations interested in creating a volunteer handbook that not only educates new volunteers, but celebrates past volunteers as well.

✓ Print the handbook in color.

✓ Include as many pictures of volunteers as possible.

✓ Use the handbook to recruit new volunteers.

✓ Include volunteer quotes.

✓ Post the handbook on a bulletin board for all volunteers and staff to see.

---

27 Create an Online Member Community ▬

Staff with the Morton Arboretum (Lisle, IL) go beyond the typical print newsletter to reach out to members through interactive online member community called tree talk.

Karin Jaros, assistant director of membership, says the goal of the online community is to get members communicating with each other, with staff and other experts who may post articles at the site.

For an organization dedicated to the mission of conserving and planting trees, creating an online community to reduce the amount of printed materials was a natural progression and in line with the goals of the organization, Jaros says.

Electronic-based Communications Allow for Updating on the Go

The online community's communications currently go to about 24,000 of the arboretum's 34,000 members electronically, says Jaros, who says the compelling component to this online community is that it can be updated at any time, even while staff are on the road.

Whenever tree talk is updated with new information (about three times a month), enrolled members receive an e-mail announcement. Members who use the RSS feed are automatically alerted to any updates to the site.

Additional benefits of creating an online community, she says, are that it gives members quick, easy access to up-to-the-minute information and a location to talk to one another. Under the tree huggers, section of the site, for example, members can interactively communicate with an arboretum scientist or staff expert about nature questions or upcoming class offerings. Video clips and content links can be added to the site to guide the member to more information about a given topic.

Online Community Allows for Interactive Communications, Contests

A significant bonus to an online community over a traditional, static newsletter is that effective tracking is possible. Jaros' experience is that activity is always strong within 48 hours of new posts or updates. Contests and surveys are also posted at this member community site, which tie into the organization's goals. For example, a photo appears asking for members to identify where it was taken on the 1,700-acre arboretum. Within 48 hours of posting the first contest, Jaros received more than 600 responses to the contest and a user survey.

"The best parts of this site are that it allows us to be really interactive, to engage in conversation and dialogue with the member, to allow them to do the same and to keep us up to date and current," Jaros says. "The minute a print newsletter goes out, it can already be out of date, especially when dealing with events."

High Traffic, Demand, Help Expand Online Communications Tool

Jaros says the initial plan was to send six new tree talk editions out to members, but due to high traffic and demand, tree talk will become a staple of member communication. The arboretum's current 2009 budgeting plans for 24 to 26 new tree talk editions.

Anyone can go to the tree talk site and view the information, but only registered members are able to post comments. Jaros says this member-only access encourages tightly focused online conversations and the bonus of new-member recruitment.

Jaros moderates the site, keeping all posts in a holding pattern until approved. Site moderating eliminates both spam and inappropriate posts to the site. She notes that she has yet to reject any post at tree talk.

"It's all about having a conversation," Jaros says. "With tree talk, we've established a format where we can have those conversations."

Jaros says the arboretum will continue to produce Seasons, the hardcopy member publication, because it has a place for those members who aren't yet online.

Source: Karin Jaros, Assistant Director of Membership, The Morton Arboretum, Lisle, IL. Phone (630) 725-2043. E-mail: KJaros@mortonarb.org

 ## 28 Be Straightforward With Your Volunteers ▬

Some volunteer managers may be reluctant to set deadlines or outline specific expectations for volunteers for fear of losing them when, in fact, just the opposite is true. Praise and recognize your volunteers for the work they do, but also let them know when they are not living up to your expectations.

Not being honest and frank with volunteers about their performance leads to confusion and apprehension. Volunteers will sense there is something wrong but, not knowing what it is, will leave. Even though volunteers don't receive paychecks, they still want to do a good job. Being honest with them about their performance will help them improve, do a better job and remain with your organization.

29 Pay Attention to Prospects' Overall Body Language

As important as it is to genuinely listen to prospects, reading their body language can also help determine what direction your message or presentation should take. While body language varies among individuals and can even have contrary meanings from one culture to another, here are some more common interpretations of typical nonverbal communications:

✓ Good eye contact with you indicates interest.

✓ Stroking one's chin may indicate your message is being evaluated.

✓ A nodding head confirms understanding.

✓ Crossed arms or legs are generally interpreted as defensiveness.

✓ Clearing one's throat may be interpreted as nervousness.

✓ Self-touching of the face may indicate concern.

✓ Rigid or jerky body movements may indicate tenseness.

Avoid interpreting stand-alone gestures, which may just be a coincidence or a person's preferred way of standing or sitting. Rather, watch for clusters of body actions that, viewed as a group, could provide you with an idea of what's going on in your prospect's mind.

If, for example, your prospect is looking away from you, keeping an eye on the clock and drumming a pen in apparent frustration or boredom, you may want to kick it up a notch by pulling out visuals, sharing a high-impact story or otherwise reengaging the apparently bored audience.

30 Frequency of Communication Matters ▬ ▬ ▬

If you're intent on moving your board from a group of symbolic figures into a group of managers who become more hands on, it's important that you maintain frequent communication with them both individually and as a group. You become both a cheerleader and a resource in pointing the way to next steps. Although some exceptional board members will assume responsibility without staff support, most need regular nudges to keep them motivated and knowledgeable about what happens next.

Here are examples of how you can provide regular communication:

1. Conduct individual phone calls to check on progress and answer any questions.

2. Distribute a weekly or monthly board memo that updates members on issues, recognizes those who have done their part and encourages everyone to keep projects moving.

3. Set up one-on-one meetings in which you question, then listen as a way to understand what motivates certain board members.

4. Provide examples of how other boards have risen to the occasion with various projects.

5. Keep your board's actions in the public eye of your entire constituency. Publish summaries of board actions in your newsletter or magazine.

Your frequency of contact with board members shows you care about their involvement and the ways in which they are contributing. It's better to have too much board contact rather than too little.

31 Philanthropy Update Spreads News, Saves Time

Staff at DePaul University (Chicago, IL) e-mail a monthly philanthropy update to select philanthropic press.

The update condenses the month's news releases into one document while familiarizing those media outlets with DePaul's fundraising and grant activities. Sent as a PDF attachment, the updates feature brief news items about grants and gifts DePaul received in the past month.

Including only brief information about each news item keeps the mailing concise and quick to read while giving recipients the opportunity to contact the university for further information, says Paul M. Baker, director of advancement communications, office of advancement.

"We want to make those publications that care about fundraising and grant activities more familiar with what we are doing at DePaul," Baker says. Combining all the news into one update rather than several separate releases throughout the month "saves us time and resources while saving the media the hassle of sorting through them all for something of interest to them."

DePaul officials currently e-mail updates to about 50 local and national philanthropic press, college and university press, and Catholic higher education press reporters (since DePaul is a Catholic university).

Baker says the e-mails have resulted in positive media coverage, including an article in the largely circulated Chicago Tribune. No one has asked to be taken off the recipient list.

Source: Paul M. Baker, Director, Advancement Communications, Office of Advancement, DePaul University, Chicago, IL. Phone (312) 362-5897. E-mail: Pbaker5@depaul.edu

32 Offer Quick Answers With Q&A Web Page ▬ ▬ ▬

Staff with the Houston Zoo (Houston, TX) save time and resources by posting answers to members' and others' frequently asked questions online.

Some of the 35 questions and answers on the zoo website's Q&A section include:

Q: *When will I get my membership card?*
A: Your membership card should arrive within two to three weeks from time of purchase. If you mail your payment in, please allow additional time for processing.

Q: *May I visit before I get my card?*
A: Sure! Just bring your photo ID and your membership receipt, or a printed copy of the e-mail confirmation if you purchased online and stop by the membership window to verify your purchase and receive your free entry to the zoo.

Q: *When does my membership expire?*
A: Your membership will expire one year from the date of purchase.

The goal in designing the member Q&A page was simple: "One-stop 'answer hopping,'" says Elizabeth Garza, director of membership. "We wanted the page to be a resource not just for Web visitors considering a first-time zoo membership purchase, but for current members as well. We review the Q&A section regularly to keep the information fresh and up to date."

Benefits of adding such a Web page include minimizing redundant questions received by phone and e-mail, Garza says. In addition, members will appreciate the ease and convenience of finding this information readily available online.

Source: Elizabeth Garza, Director of Membership, Houston Zoo, Houston, TX. E-mail: egarza@houstonzoo.org

33 Personal Phone Calls Build Rapport With Volunteers ▬

Coming into a volunteer management position when the person you're replacing was well loved can be difficult. Lakeesha Campbell, volunteer coordinator, Presbyterian Hospice and Palliative Care (Charlotte, NC), has a simple, proven way to build rapport:

Every two weeks, Campbell calls each of her 50 volunteers. She keeps calls low key and personal, asking how the volunteer is and if he/she needs anything from her.

Campbell says her predecessor advised her to make the calls to build and maintain personal relationships with the volunteers. She admits that at first she thought there was no way she could find time for 50 personal phone calls every other week. But, by splitting the list up and making about 10 calls a day, she can do so easily.

The personal calls let Campbell stay close with volunteers and offer a chance just to say "hello," rather than just calling when she has a volunteer need to fill.

Source: Lakeesha Campbell, Volunteer Coordinator, Presbyterian Hospice and Palliative Care, Charlotte, NC. Phone (704) 384-3527. E-mail: lcampbell@novanthealth.org

35 Rap Session Lets Members Speak Out ▬ ▬ ▬

At least twice yearly, hold a rap session. Invite members to meet in small groups with the director and/or board members in an informal setting. Freely, but positively, discuss problems, obstacles, morale. Brainstorm together, share ideas. Make a rule that those who present a problem must also offer a probable solution.

Rap sessions empower members, create unity, offer a chance to vent and employ personal creativity. Managed wisely, they are a tremendous asset.

34 Send a Personalized Letter With Your Annual Fund Brochure ▬

Because staff and faculty of St. Lawrence University (Canton, NY) believe in the power of direct peer-to-peer contact, they include a personalized letter when sending brochures, says Kimberly May Hissong, director of alumni and parent programs office.

"Our university is known for its personal interaction," says Hissong. "Our alums have come to expect personalization, and will even contact us when they receive a stand-alone brochure to point out that it wasn't sent with a letter."

Their annual fund letters are typically signed by a class chair, the annual fund chair or Hissong.

"We provide our volunteers with a template that includes a few paragraphs containing the key messages about giving and participation that we want to get across," she says. "They are asked to personalize the letter by writing introductory and closing paragraphs."

Each spring semester they send a letter and Choices brochure. Instead of personalizing the brochure for each alum, says Hissong, the brochure allows the alum to personalize their gifts. "The brochure shows visually and with text how alumni can personalize their annual fund gifts," she says. "It provides six or seven choices for making their gift."

Hissong says they send on average four annual fund appeals to between 15,000 and 18,000 alums each year. Each mailing receives a 2 to 4 percent response rate.

Source: Kimberly May Hissong, Director of Alumni and Parent Programs Office, St. Lawrence University, Canton, NY. Phone (315) 229-5837. E-mail: khissong@stlawu.edu

36 Communicating With a Virtual Volunteer ▬

As technology grows, so does the number of persons who volunteer or coordinate their volunteer assignments in a virtual environment.

Virtual volunteers may perform some or all of their volunteer duties online, such as conducting research, designing a website or translating a document into another language. Or they may get their assignments via website and e-mail contacts, and perform the service at their home or in a client's home, such as sewing quilts or providing respite care to an in-home caregiver.

Virtual volunteers may also be active online, for example, staffing a chat room or overseeing an online discussion group for a nonprofit.

Donna Stutler, volunteer resource director, Damar Services (Indianapolis, IN), a nonprofit that serves developmentally disabled children and adults — has tapped into a new resource by creating virtual volunteer positions.

Stutler uses e-mail exclusively to contact all of her volunteers. She e-mails them about job assignments, checks in with e-mail and even sends thank-yous through e-mail. "It works out great!" she says of the online method of identifying, screening, assigning tasks to and supervising volunteers.

Since more and more volunteers are computer savvy, Stutler says she needed to make changes to adapt her volunteer program. "I needed to be more creative, because I know that's where we're heading," she says.

Stutler created all of her virtual volunteer positions, selecting tasks that people could complete off-site, such as assembling newsletters for staff and volunteers or mending clients' clothing. She posts the volunteer opportunities online at VolunteerMatch.com.

Source: Donna Stutler, Volunteer Resource Director, Damar Services, Indianapolis, IN. Phone (371) 856-5201. E-mail: donnas@damar.org

37 Inside Hadley Helps to Build, Strengthen Relationships ▬

After reading about giving societies in The Major Gifts Report, The Hadley School for the Blind (Winnetka, IL) established two giving societies in 2004 — the President's Society, to acknowledge donors of $1,000 to $4,999, and the Heritage Society, to acknowledge donors of $5,000 and more.

To give these societies some degree of exclusivity and provide members with more frequent updates, they created an insider's newsletter called Inside Hadley, says Thomas Tobin, vice president, development and communications.

"Inside Hadley makes it easier to communicate with major supporters, actively cultivate a relationship and keep them informed about the school," says Tobin. "The newsletter also showcases how we utilize our higher level donor gifts."

About 425 people currently receive the quarterly newsletter, including current donors at the $1,000 and above level, prospective donors and the school's board of trustees. Begun as a one-color Word document, the newsletter was redesigned in the past year as a four-color, says Tobin, a change that has greatly increased its visual interest and readability.

The newsletter includes highlights of special events or news about Hadley; upcoming events; a recap of fundraising goals; student growth and updates on courses and programs; strategic plan updates; and a tax legislation recap. Photos and graphics are used whenever feasible, he says, and all copy is kept short and easy to read.

"Our donors stay more vested in Hadley since they receive regular information on the school," says Tobin. "Last year, gifts from President and Heritage Society members totaled 18 percent of gifts received. We attribute this to not only the newsletter but more personal attention the donors receive from the school. For example, a donor who had given

$100 a year for several years was put on the prospect list and began receiving Inside Hadley. This year he gave $1,000 and became a new President's Society member."

Source: Thomas Tobin, Vice President of Development and Communications, The Hadley School for the Blind, Winnetka, IL. Phone (847) 784-2765. E-mail: tobin@hadley.edu

Content not available in this edition

38 E-mail Marketing Offers Cost-effective Communication ■ ■ ■

An inexpensive way to improve communication and to increase membership is through e-mail marketing.

Within the year Sarasota Film Society started using Constant Contact — an e-mail marketing service — its membership grew 50 percent, from 4,000 to 6,000 members. Robert Macadaeg, director of marketing and publicity, Sarasota Film Society, attributes much of the growth to e-mail marketing, "which has helped us to be at the top of people's minds."

A weekly e-mail newsletter replaced the society's print newsletter.

"We used to send it out every other month, but our film schedules are volatile," Macadaeg says. "Paper wasn't a good format. E-mail gives us the opportunity to have an almost real-time conversation with customers and give them valuable information that doesn't change as the weeks go by."

Along with publishing a weekly newsletter, the society uses Constant Contact to send renewal reminders for memberships and special events announcements.

Constant Contact allows associations and nonprofits to communicate quickly and affordably with their members, donors and sponsors, says Gail Goodman, Constant Contact CEO. Paper and postage costs can make direct mail campaigns too costly in time and money for many organizations.

"Instant response and the ability to measure the

Macadaeg's tips for using e-mail marketing:

- Use more pictures than text.
- Keep content short, sweet and useful.
- Deliver some value with the message.
- Don't send your newsletter more than weekly.
- Deliver weekly, but only if you have something valuable to share.
- Grow your list by always offering your members a way to sign up when you have access to them.

success of campaigns are other unique benefits afforded by e-mail marketing," Goodman says. "Immediately after nonprofits and associations send their newsletters, their subscribers can reply or make a donation. And with the automated tracking tools built into the Constant Contact system, users can easily measure the effectiveness of each campaign and use the metrics to modify future campaigns for greater success."

Few technical skills are required to use e-mail marketing. "There are more than 100 professional e-mail templates to choose from and no HTML skills are needed to get to work immediately on crafting a campaign," Goodman says.

Organizations can create highly customized newsletters with Constant Contacts' image-hosting feature, allowing users to upload their own photos and graphics.

Constant Contact offers free, live customer support 12 hours daily, Monday through Friday, as well as live chat and e-mail. E-mail marketing programs start at $15 per month. Constant Contact offers a free 60-day trial, so clients can experience the program before buying.

Sources: Robert Macadaeg, Director of Marketing and Publicity, Sarasota Film Society, Sarasota, FL. Phone (941) 364-8662. E-mail: Robert@filmsociety.org
Gail Goodman, CEO, Constant Contact, Waltham, MA. Phone (781) 472-8150. E-mail: ggoodman@constantcontact.com

39 Four Key Elements ■ ■ ■ To Successful Communications

Effective communication is essential in managing volunteers. Here are four key elements to successful communications with your volunteers:

Clarity. Clearly explain what you want done clearly. Don't assume anything.

Consistency. Volunteer managers need to be consistent in their communications. Don't set a policy one week and change it the next, at least without an explanation.

Conflict. It's important that a volunteer manager deal with conflict and/or poor performance issues immediately. Give regular feedback on performance and encourage volunteer feedback.

Courage. Have the courage to be honest when communicating with volunteers. If you need to criticize a volunteer's performance, don't take the easy way out and write a letter or e-mail. Talk to the person face to face and give him/her a chance to respond.

40 Practice Your Presentation Delivery ■ ■ ■

Even if you're a veteran development pro, it doesn't hurt to hone your one-on-one presentation skills. These presentation exercises will help improve your actual delivery:

1. Write out a presentation summary. Doing so forces you to identify key messages you want to convey.

2. Use notecards to develop a presentation outline, then practice with and without them.

3. Go through your presentation, first with a colleague, then with someone less familiar with your nonprofit. Select someone who will give you honest feedback.

4. Prepare a list of possible questions and objections. Review each of them and develop convincing responses.

Although there is no substitute for the real thing, the more you plan and prepare for important presentations, the more convincing you will be to would-be donors.

E-newsletter Stewards
Donor Relationships ▪

Has your development office considered sending an e-newsletter to your donors as a strategic form of communication?

In January, officials with the Oklahoma State University (OSU) Foundation (Stillwater, OK) launched donorlink, a donor e-newsletter distributed to donors who have given any dollar amount in the previous calendar year, as a means of keeping them connected to the foundation.

"We are not using it as a solicitation tool to garner additional gifts but rather as a stewardship piece," says Lisa Frein, communications specialist. "We want to keep the OSU Foundation at the forefront of our donors' minds by providing constant and consistent communication on charitable giving and philanthropy to OSU through various mediums."

Frein says the e-newsletter enables them to cultivate relationships with donors at smaller giving levels that do not qualify them to receive other foundation publications.

Before OSU staff launched donorlink, the foundation's CEO sent donors e-mails announcing the e-newsletter and asking them to watch for it in their inboxes.

Frein says the quarterly e-newsletter was sent to more than 18,000 donors fitting the criteria for which the foundation office had e-mail addresses. OnMarketer, the e-mail distribution service hired by the foundation, reported that of the messages sent, 15 percent (2,740) were opened by recipients, with the number of total opens at 5,588, nearly double the number of opens from recipients.

Frein says that the number of total opens "was perhaps the most exciting number to us because it meant people were forwarding and sharing our e-newsletter with others."

Cost to implement the e-newsletter was minimal, with all of the content, design and setup done in-house by the marketing and communication team. The only external cost is a $70 monthly fee for onMarketer's service.

Source: Lisa Frein, Communications Specialist, Oklahoma State University Foundation, Stillwater, OK. Phone (405) 385-5115.
E-mail: lfrein@osugiving.com

Content not available in this edition

 ### Use Positive Language
To Change Behavior ▪

Many times when we have to criticize a volunteer, we start out with a positive comment followed by a "but" and ending with a critical statement such as, "I really liked the way you arranged that display, but the others need attention."

The volunteer may at first be uplifted by the positive comment. But then the word "but" may leave him/her wondering whether the first statement was really sincere.

Next time trying changing the word "but" to "and." For example, "I really liked the way you arranged that display and if you put the same effort into the others, the whole area will look terrific."

43 Communications Tip ▪ ▪ ▪

Don't overlook the power of a personal letter to members or would-be members. With the proliferation of e-mail, a personal letter arriving by mail is more of an attention-grabber than in years past.

44 Get the Most Out of Volunteer Surveys ▬ ▬ ▬

The Park Nicollet Health Services (St. Louis Park, MN) created a volunteer survey that is simple and straightforward, yet provides meaningful results. An employee survey was transformed into a volunteer template that can be easily updated. The two-page survey includes brief questions about background, length of service and age range; sense of comfort with the hospital's mission; work support received; and their overall assessment of the organization.

Questions are short, with a single box for volunteer comments. Each section serves a particular goal, for example, whether volunteers would like greater involvement in decisions affecting their work. Managers are asked to make changes based on the survey. Subsequent surveys will help determine whether volunteer concerns were addressed.

Volunteers also help enter the responses in an Excel spreadsheet. Results are published on the front page of the volunteer newsletter and made available at the annual mandatory education training. Sharing survey results helps volunteers better understand how their survey participation assists the organization.

Source: Linda Velez, Director, Volunteer Services, Park Nicollet Health Services, St. Louis Park, MN. Phone (952) 993-5086. E-mail: Linda.velez@parknicollet.com

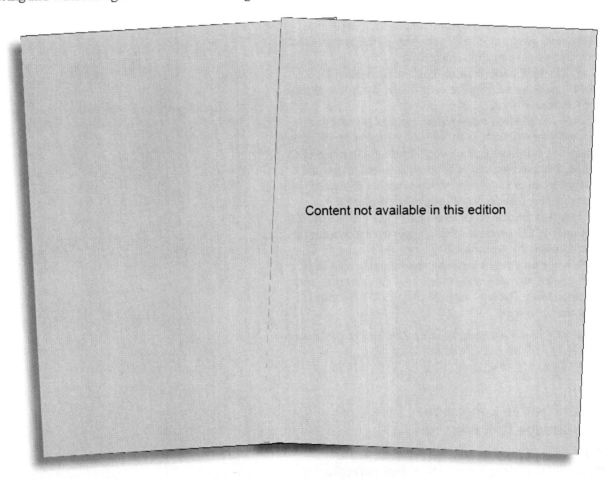

Content not available in this edition

45 Create a Members-only Hotline for Easy Updates ▬

It can be time consuming and expensive to notify each member of an important update or emergency. Establishing an informational hotline takes the burden off your shoulders while still providing a useful resource to your members.

Consider setting up a members-only hotline, preferably toll-free, that allows members to call in and access up-to-date information. One or two staff members can be designated to update the hotline's message regularly to keep members informed. Depending on the type of phone system you use, it may be possible for your staff to update the hotline from outside your office, allowing easier access and more frequent updates. Members will have access to the information they need in a way that's convenient and cost effective.

Let Members Tell Others Why They Belong ▬ ▬ ▬

When officials with the Texas Library Association (TLA) of Austin, TX set up the organization's official website, they asked members to submit testimonials to be posted on the site.

To ensure testimonials reflected the diversity of their membership, they considered members' ethnicity, library type (school, academic, public or special), age and geographic location, says Kathy Pustejovsky, conference and membership manager.

"We wanted to use the testimonials as a membership recruitment tool," Pustejovsky says. "I've found that word-of-mouth is the best advertising there is, and it really personalizes the membership process for new and/or renewing members."

The testimonials also give credibility to the organization and its mission, she says.

"In the 22 years that I've been with the association, TLA has been very fortunate to not have suffered a decrease in membership even though the economy has not been kind to this group of educators. Our members see their TLA membership as a commitment to their profession, and not just a repository for their dues dollars. We are very dependent on an active volunteer base, so many of our members get involved and stay involved. They develop lifelong friendships as well as a networking source.

"Testimonials are helpful in making a member feel like part of a family, and not just a membership number in a database."

Source: Kathy J. Pustejovsky, Conference and Membership Manager, Texas Library Association, Austin, TX. Phone (512) 328-8852. E-mail: kathyp@txla.org

---

Texas Library Association Member Testimonials:
I belong to TLA because ...

"...I believe in libraries as valuable contributors to a civilized society, and I believe TLA helps make librarians strong and knowledgeable so they can do their jobs better."

Bonnie Juergens
AMIGOS Bibliographic Council

"...It is the only organization which can speak effectively for and to all kinds of Texas librarians. TLA's legislative efforts have met with repeated success. TLA's conference programming and exhibits are unparalleled among state associations and are a source of valuable information and continuing education. I encourage every Texas librarian to become a member."

Al Cage, Stephen F. Austin
State University

"...Amistades, compartimiento de ideas, y motivacin (friendships, sharing of ideas and motivation)."

Dorothea Castan
Corpus Christi Public Library

 ## Respect the Power of Listening ▬

Major gift fundraising is more about listening than talking. In fact, solicitors who talk too much tend to fail, says Andy Robinson (Plainfield, VT), trainer, consultant and author of "Big Gifts for Small Groups."

"Novices are the worst offenders because they're filled with nervous energy," says Robinson. Uncomfortable with silence, they "work doubly hard to carry the conversation. They mistakenly believe that ... armed with the perfect case, they can talk somebody into giving, so they obsess about getting the language right."

He says development officers can actually talk people out of giving. To prevent that from happening, "listen" someone into giving by asking good questions and being fully present in the conversation. He points to fundraising guru Jerry Panas who calls this "listening the gift."

"Fundraising isn't about money — it's about relationships," says Robinson. "How do you feel when friends or family talk too much and monopolize the conversation? Or when they get excited about their interests and passions and problems, but never ask about yours? Would you rather listen to a monologue or join a dialogue?"

He advises asking these questions when meeting with donors or prospects:

- Why are you interested in our work?
- What is your experience with our issue? Has someone you known been affected?
- (For current donors): Last year, you gave $___. Why did you do it? What is it about our work that moves you?
- What are your favorite causes? Why?
- When you make a donation, how do you like to be acknowledged?

"Remember, your job is to stimulate dialogue, and the best way to do that is to ask questions," says Robinson. "People like to talk about themselves, so make it easy. The more they talk, the better your chance of getting the gift — not because you manipulate them, but because you're genuinely interested in their point of view. If you know what motivates them, you'll be a more responsive partner."

Source: Andy Robinson, Trainer, Consultant and Author, Plainfield, VT. Phone (802) 479-7365. E-mail: andyfund@earthlink.net

---

Article Designation Key: Donors ▬▬▬ Members ▬▬▬ Volunteers ▬▬▬

48 College's Annual President's Report Doubles as Stewardship, Fundraising Tool ▪

Taking a tried-and-true concept to a new level can pay off in increased awareness, fresh vision and — ultimately — significant financial support for a nonprofit organization.

For seven years, staff at Agnes Scott College (Decatur, GA) have published an annual president's report that combines the annual report of donors, a brief annual report and editorial copy, says Jennifer Bryon Owen, interim director of communications.

For the latest report, Owen says, they went all out to produce a piece that gives an emotional introduction of the president's newly adopted seven-year strategic plan.

"We wanted to introduce the strategic plan with a gripping, beautiful piece that would get people's attention," she says.

The stand-alone, 48-page publication, which feels like a magazine, is printed in color on 80-pound matte paper. It opens with a letter from the college president and ends with an honor roll of donors. The center pages feature the college's new strategic plan.

Published in December 2007, the report was mailed to 14,000 alumni, as well as peer colleges. Additional copies are used as donor cultivation tools by the college's fundraising staff and distributed by the president at speaking engagements.

Susan Constantine, director of corporate and foundation relations, says she uses the publication to help donors learn what the strategic plan is all about and to show them the number and breadth of donors to the college. The well-designed, attractive piece is particularly useful at meetings with corporate and foundation donors, she says. "It has been a great tool in letting people know what kind of college Agnes Scott is."

While college staff didn't design the piece as a direct fundraising tool, they do include a business reply envelope (BRE) with it.

"We see it as a cultivation piece and communication tool," says Owen. "We hope that it will encourage those individuals who don't give to give, and those donors who do give to increase the size of their gift."

While the number of donations that come from the report's BRE are usually fewer than those received from the college's twice-yearly magazine and thrice-yearly tabloid newspaper, she says, the average gift is larger.

"We believe the donor list, combined with our editorial focus, makes the value of the president's report far greater than just the amount of donations it yields, although the donations are still important," says Owen. "We see our publications as being supportive of our fundraising, and work with our development staff in crafting pieces they can use."

Sources: Jennifer Bryon Owen, Interim Director of Communications; Susan Constantine, Director of Corporate and Foundation Relations; Agnes Scott College, Decatur, GA. Phone (404) 471-6301 or (404) 471-6056. E-mail: jowen@agnesscott.edu or sconstantine@agnesscott.edu

The annual president's report for Agnes Scott College (Decatur, GA) is an effective tool to share the college's strategic plan and vision.

Content not available in this edition

49   Discussion Boards Useful for Volunteers and Managers ▪▪ ▪▪ ▪▪

Can a discussion board work for your agency? Big Brothers Big Sisters of Greater Pittsburgh (Pittsburgh, PA) is one of a handful of the nation's BBBS agencies to start up a discussion board for its volunteers.

The interactive Web-based board provides a forum to Bigs (adult volunteers who mentor to youth in a big brother or sister/little brother or sister relationship) to communicate with each other and the agency. They can post questions on subjects such as money issues, suggestions of outings with their Littles and how to handle it when the sibling of a Little wants to be part of the outings.

The online discussion board is of value not only to volunteers who can bounce ideas off of one another, but also to staff, says Cheryl Jones, special services coordinator. She says that staff monitor the discussion, and if a volunteer is found to be posting something inappropriate, staff remove it and contact the volunteer to discuss the reasons for removal.

The online discussion board is also a great way to follow up training efforts with the volunteers, Jones says, as staff can address questions that arise on the discussion board and use the topics for volunteer support.

Jones can also check what the volunteers are reading on the site. Each Big is given his/her own password to the site. Only Bigs and staff can access, read and post to the discussion board.

Jones drives the volunteers to the board by posting valuable information Bigs need to know, like upcoming events and tickets available to those events. This helps drive down the amount of time Jones spends e-mailing reminders to volunteers.

One tip Jones has about starting up your own discussion board is making sure you work out the technical bugs. Because it is a protected site just for volunteers and staff, firewall bugs and other security issues must be addressed. Also, she says, make sure the discussion board is protected, yet still easily accessible from any computer.

Source: Cheryl Jones, Special Services Coordinator, Big Brothers Big Sisters of Greater Pittsburgh, Pittsburgh, PA. Phone (412) 363-6100. E-mail: cjones@bbbspgh.org

50   Blogs Great Way to Get Your Message to Wider Audience ▪▪ ▪▪ ▪▪

The American Constitution Society for Law & Policy (ACS) of Washington, DC, launched a Web log, or blog, in 2004 to join in on the discourse regarding legal and public policy that already existed in the blogging community, says David Lyle, deputy director. Currently, the ACS blog has five to six posts a day and some 30,000 unique visitors per month.

"The blog allows our members and supporters to participate in conversations about legal and public policy issues and to promote ideas that matter to them," Lyle says. "Being involved in these conversations raises the profile of our organization. Since we invite both members and nonmembers to post to the blog, it's also a great way to engage with existing members and recruit new members and supporters."

People must be specifically asked to post to the blog but anyone can comment on posts, he says: "By retaining editorial control over the posts, we can stay more consistently true to our mission. Those who post ... become more interested in our organization, and tend to follow up and become members or otherwise stay engaged."

The ACS has a team of volunteer law student editors to manage daily blog posts, solicit posts by members and nonmembers and promote the blog by having other blogs link to it and send traffic to the site. The editors also post to the site themselves.

A big part of the blogging culture is linking to other blogs, says Lyle: "It's a culture of reciprocity; you link to them and they link to you and that's how you get traffic to your site." The ACS promotes the blog in a weekly e-newsletter by pointing out the week's most interesting posts, inviting members to post and telling them how.

For organizations that want to start a blog, Lyle has this advice:

"Don't think that 'If you build it, they will come.' You need to have something to say that at least some subset of people are interested in. As with anything else, you tend to get out of it what you invest in it. If you have an audience for what you're saying and aggressively promote it to that audience, you'll have pretty good success."

Source: David Lyle, Deputy Director, American Constitution Society for Law & Policy, Washington DC. Phone (202) 393-6181. E-mail: dlyle@acslaw.org. Website: www.acslaw.org

> The American
> Constitution Society
> for Law & Policy
> online diary:
> www.acsblog.org

51   Listening Skills Tip ▪▪ ▪▪ ▪▪

- Recognize that the way in which a message is being conveyed is sometimes as important as the words. Pay attention to the speed of speech, breathing patterns, voice tone and pitch to more fully comprehend what's being shared.

52 Include a Detailed Calendar of Events Online ▬ ▬ ▬

Officials with the Philadelphia Museum of Art (Philadelphia, PA) have found an inexpensive way to keep members up to date on the latest events and event details.

M.E. Bissert, communications coordinator, says the museum decided to add the user-friendly members' calendar in 2006 when they redesigned their website.

"Since many of our members utilize the Internet as an information resource, it was important for us to provide this service," says Bissert.

The calendar, which is updated as needed to provide members with up-to-the-minute information, is accessible to the museum's approximately 50,000 members. It features members-only events, programs, tours and public programs, including concerts, art history courses, lectures, family events and tours.

Bissert says the calendar also serves as a form of promotion. "Visitors are able to browse months in advance and view detailed program descriptions. They can search by event type. Having this information easily accessible creates interest and a buzz. We have included a 'forward to a friend' button, which sends the event information to a friend of the website visitor."

The institution also mails a monthly printed publication to their membership base to reach members who may not regularly use computers.

Source: M.E. Bissert, Communications Coordinator, Membership and Visitors Services Department, Philadelphia Museum of Art, Philadelphia, PA. Phone (215) 684-7853.
E-mail: mbissert@philamuseum.org

53 Informality Sometimes Fosters Good Communications ▬ ▬ ▬

Sharing a cup of coffee and a donut with a friend is often the best moment to share the events transpiring in your life. This concept can also be applied to volunteer support groups.

Jennifer Cunningham, volunteer coordinator, Gaston Hospice (Gastonia, NC), attributes the success of quarterly volunteer meetings to the informality and fellowship experienced by all participants. Openness and informality foster interaction among the volunteers.

"We offered formal luncheon meetings in the past. Volunteers told us that they preferred to get together and talk," says Cunningham.

The agenda of each meeting covers a specific topic, while Cunningham also responds to volunteer questions and concerns. Veteran volunteers serve as mentors by sharing their experiences and offering advice during the meetings.

Although the meetings are informal, Cunningham uses them to her advantage. These sessions are intended to help volunteers who are grieving for patients under their care, but also provide continuing education. For example, while one meeting will focus on death and dying, another will focus on polices and procedures, like setting boundaries with patients.

The volunteers suggest topics. Cunningham also considers current volunteer trends. If a large number of volunteers have lost patients during a particular quarter, she'll hold a special meeting to address their emotions and concerns.

Early morning and early evening meetings attract a larger turnout. Cunningham often alternates between these times to ensure that all of her volunteers can attend.

Source: Jennifer Cunningham, Volunteer Coordinator, Gaston Hospice, Gastonia, NC. Phone (704) 861-8405.
E-mail: cunningh@gmh.org

54 Direct a Newsletter to Sponsors, Would-be Sponsors ▬

To convince more businesses to support your organization and encourage existing donors to give at higher levels, consider pursuing sponsorships rather than outright gifts.

To cultivate new and increased sponsorships, consider a monthly or quarterly newsletter directed to existing and would-be sponsors. To keep costs in line, you might want to make it an e-newsletter.

What might such a sponsors' newsletter include in the way of content? Here's a sampling of the possibilities:

• New or enhanced sponsorship benefits.

• Profiles of current sponsors and what they are underwriting.

• Recognition of newly enlisted sponsors.

• Brief descriptions of sponsorship opportunities.

• Features about how a particular sponsorship is impacting your organization's programs and services.

• A regular message from the chair of your sponsorship advisory council.

• Announcements of upcoming sponsors-only events.

• Messages from those who are benefiting from sponsorship support.

• A calendar of upcoming events for your organization that spotlights sponsor-funded or supported happenings.

• A request to forward the e-newsletter to others in their circle of influence.

55 Forms Work Together to Communicate Needs Between Staff and Volunteers ▪

Content not available in this edition

When groups call to volunteer or staff come to you in need of a hand, do you have a list of tasks at your fingertips? Or do you scramble to fill their needs?

The more organized and ready you are when volunteers step forth, the better for everyone involved.

Mandi Lindner, community relations coordinator, United Community Center (Milwaukee, WI), created two forms to help define both what the volunteer and staff needs are for group projects: The Volunteer Project Request Form and Volunteer Project Interest Form, both shown at left.

The volunteer project interest form, used when a group calls, is available on the organization's website, (www.unitedcc.org) for companies to download or to view as Lindner fills it out over the phone with them.

The interest form asks for contact information, plus information on scope of project the group has in mind (e.g., number of volunteers, age range, availability, skills possessed and what group of clients the volunteers wish to work with — seniors, adults or students).

The volunteer project request form enables staff program coordinators to communicate with Lindner when they have ideas or needs for volunteers.

The form asks staff to list how many volunteers they will need, when the volunteers will be needed and for what type of project or event. It also asks the minimum age of volunteers, their responsibilities and supplies required.

Lindner says the forms work together efficiently. She keeps them in a book at her desk so when a group expresses an interest to volunteer or a staff member has a request, she can quickly look and immediately fill the need.

The interest form also helps her track what volunteer opportunities work best with what groups. For instance, knowing that school groups enjoy working with seniors while corporations enjoy special events helps her match those interests with needs.

In the 18 months she has used the forms, Lindner says she has seen a significant reduction in both the stress and workload that creating group projects can bring. She sends quarterly updates to each program coordinator to remind them to fill out the request forms.

Source: Mandi Lindner, Community Relations Coordinator, United Community Center, Milwaukee, WI. Phone (414) 384-3100. E-mail: mlindner@unitedcc.org. Website: www.unitedcc.org

Article Designation Key: Donors ▓▓▓▓   Members ▓▓▓▓   Volunteers ▓▓▓▓

56 Boost End-of-year Giving With Online Wish List ■

Wish lists are tried-and-true ways to generate targeted support. With the holiday season fast approaching, now is the ideal time to create and post an online wish list of items, projects and services for supporters to fund with their end-of-year gifts.

If you already have an online wish list, add some attention-getting items and get the word out about year-end opportunities through print and electronic communications.

Wish Lists May Be Basic Laundry Lists Or Highly Detailed Documents

Some organizations' wish lists include a simple checklist of needs (e.g., copy paper, postage stamps). Others go on to include a price estimate and brief description. Still others design highly detailed wish lists complete with photos and how the items will benefit the nonprofit's mission and more.

The Berrien County Council for Children/The Children's Assessment Center (St. Joseph, MI) has a two-part wish list accessible by a direct link on its website's navigation bar (http://berrienchild.org/wish_list.html).

In addition to expected, less expensive wish-list items, such as printer cartridges and cleaning supplies, the nonprofit lists more creative ways to help, such as purchasing or partially funding an internal voicemail system ($3,000) or sponsoring brochure printing costs ($2,000).

Tia Miller, executive director, says since creating the online wish list in 2007, they have received a number of items, including office desks and children's supplies. She recommends being as specific as possible and including a price estimate to help guarantee you receive exactly what you need.

Another organization finding success with an online wish list is the Animal Medical Center (New York, NY). The wish list (shown in part at left) has brought in about $12,000 worth of gifts and goods in its first year, says Brandi Perrow, associate director of development.

The organization's wish list includes a photo, reason item is needed, cost and, if applicable, the amount raised toward the purchase of that item.

For example, a picture of a severely obese dog accompanies this text: "Fitness Maintenance for Fido. Some of our animal friends carry a little too much around the waist. Help the AMC obtain weight scales to monitor and manage obesity and

diabetes. Needs: 1. Price Each: $1,200 ($300 raised)."

Offer Wished-for Items From Small to Large Price Ranges

When offering a wish list, Perrow says it is important to include items of varying costs to appeal to donors from all financial backgrounds.

What is the appeal of a wish list? "I think donors feel more connected when they can buy something on your list. They are fulfilling one of your wishes," Perrow says. "Donors are getting very savvy, and they are concerned with where their money goes.... There is a comfort level with knowing exactly where their money is going and how it is being used."

Sources: Tia Miller, Executive Director, Berrien County Council for Children/The Children's Assessment Center, St. Joseph, MI. Phone (269) 556-9640. E-mail: tmiller@berrienchild.org Brandi Perrow, Associate Director of Development, The Animal Medical Center, New York, NY. Phone (212) 329-8662. E-mail: brandi.perrow@amcny.org. Website: www.amcny.org

Content not available in this edition

 57 Create an Accomplishments Brochure ■

Whenever your organization's year concludes, be sure to develop a brochure listing all volunteer accomplishments from the previous year. Such a brochure can be used to:

1. Recognize existing volunteers.
2. Recruit new volunteers.
3. Convince staff and top management of volunteers' collective contributions.

 58 Hone Your Listening Skills ■ ■ ■

How good of a listener are you?

Your members will feel more empowered if you focus on listening to them rather than talking. As they warm up, they may share more personal information — likes, dislikes, personal interests and more — that will help to strengthen your relationship with them.

59 Include Member Interviews in Newsletter, Magazine ▪▪ ▪▪ ▪▪

Looking for a fun way to get to know your members? Include lighthearted personal interviews with them in your membership newsletter or magazine.

Officials with the Sanibel & Captiva Islands Chamber of Commerce (Sanibel Island, FL) began including member interviews in its news magazine in 2007.

They print and distribute some 2,000 copies of the magazine every two months.

"This feature came about through one of many creative brainstorming sessions between my husband and me," says Bridgit Stone-Budd, director of marketing.

"I wanted something light and fun, but also informative for our members," Stone-Budd says. "Through research and experience, I've realized that retaining readership is fueled by two things: local interest stories and member photos. Fellow members and business owners enjoy reading about each other."

Interview subjects answer 10 questions created by Stone-Budd. She draws from a pool of questions she crafted, but, she notes, "I do use some particular ones over and over again because I get hilarious answers."

Some of her favorite questions include:

- What did you want to be when you grew up?

- Boxers or briefs?

- Do you like Spam?

To determine which member to interview, she says, "I pick different groups of members, sometimes accommodations, sometimes the board of directors, retail, restaurants, services, etc. Then I e-mail the interview questions to about 10 to 15 in the group in hopes that I can pick at least five good/juicy ones per issue."

When creating interview questions, use a mix of serious and silly questions to create a more dynamic interview.

Source: Bridgit Stone-Budd, Director of Marketing, Sanibel & Captiva Islands Chamber of Commerce, Sanibel Island, FL. Phone (239) 472-8255. Website: www.sanibel-captiva.biz

Content not available in this edition

60 Web Logs Can Convey Leaders' Voices ▪▪ ▪▪ ▪▪

Online Web log diaries and their audio counterparts, podcasts, can be useful to major gifts fundraisers struggling to find a voice for their institution's leadership within their community.

Many development officers — especially among smaller, grassroots organizations — lament the lack of voice their executive directors or board members have within the local media, professional groups or the community at large. A regular Web log can provide that voice and at no cost to the organization.

For development purposes, perhaps the most effective use of a Web log is as a sounding board for executive leadership. An executive director or board member can post daily, weekly or monthly updates on the organization's vision, fundraising achievements and accomplishments. The Web log can be open to the public or restricted to a list of invited visitors, such as volunteers or major donors. These online communities of Web log subscribers inspire a camaraderie users can experience any time they log onto the site.

Another benefit of using regular, Web-based communication is that anyone with access can post to the Web log. If the executive director who usually provides the message is indisposed, the development director can sit in as a guest or even compose that message under the executive director's signature. A Web log can even be written on a regular basis by the development director and attributed to anyone else to whom you wish to give a voice, such as the board chairman.

Web logs are easy to use and to access, making them a good tool for even the most technologically challenged. This ease of use is of obvious benefit for the Web log's author, who need spend just minutes a day composing a message. With a few clicks of the mouse, the message is posted.

For the user — your audience — reading a Web log is even easier. A link to the Web log can be stored on a computer desktop for easy, one-click access.

For more on a blog and how it's used, visit www.blogbasics.com.

To get started visit www.blogger.com.

61 Placement Questionnaire Addresses Volunteer Satisfaction ■

You and your staff invest plenty of time and resources into recruiting and training volunteers. But what do you do to measure their satisfaction levels or address concerns?

Volunteer services staff with Saint Joseph Hospital's (Lexington, KY) use a one-page placement questionnaire to measure how satisfied new volunteers are with their assignments. Jamine Hamner, volunteer coordinator, says they developed the form six years ago after realizing they rarely saw many volunteers once they began volunteering, either because of the placement location or the volunteer's shift.

Hamner mails or e-mails the placement questionnaire, shown here, with a cover letter to volunteers two months into an assignment. She reviews responses and forwards them to the director or unit manager to which the volunteer is assigned.

"If a volunteer is not happy with his or her placement, we can notify the staff so they can work with the volunteer to make the placement better or we can reassign the volunteer to a more suitable placement," she says.

She estimates her office sends 300 questionnaires annually and sees about half returned, noting that the use of e-mail has resulted in a slight increase in returns.

Source: Jamine Hamner, Coordinator, Volunteer Services, Saint Joseph Hospital, Lexington, KY. Phone (859) 313-1290. E-mail: hamnerja@sjhlex.org

Content not available in this edition

62 Why a Quarterly Newsletter Makes Sense ■

Whether you produce it on your own or outsource the job through a planned gifts consultant, distributing a quarterly planned gifts newsletter makes good sense. Here's why:

✓ **It helps to position your organization in the minds of would-be donors.** There are plenty of nonprofit organizations vying for planned gifts. The absence of ongoing planned gift messages will result in missed opportunities.

✓ **It allows you to educate would-be and existing donors.** A periodic newsletter enables you to provide constituents with technical information about various types of planned gifts and the benefits of each.

✓ **It supplements your efforts to build relationships.** Personal visits, phone calls, events and more all help to nurture relationships that will either result in planned gifts or help to solidify existing gifts.

✓ **It can be used to inspire others and recognize donors' generosity.** A planned gifts newsletter enables you to recognize planned gift donors and underscore the impact of gifts that have been realized.

63 Keep Members Informed With a Phone Tree ■ ■

Consider creating a member phone tree to use in the case of a cancelled event or other scheduling conflict. Such a tool will cut down on time needed for staff to notify members and ensure all members are informed of the change in a timely manner.

For example, if an event is cancelled at the last minute, it may be impossible to call several hundred members in less than two hours to let them know of the change. However, if you break your membership down into a handful of groups and create mini-phone trees, you can streamline these outreach efforts.

Designate several members in advance to start the phone tree for their particular group and reach out to them immediately upon learning of a major change, such as a last-minute cancellation. Each member then makes one call to the next member on the list, passing on the news, and so on, until all members have been informed. If a member cannot directly reach the next person on the list, he/she should skip ahead and call the next member in line to ensure that the phone tree is not broken.

In addition to the phone tree, send a mass e-mail as well as a text message to all members for whom you have appropriate e-mail addresses and cell phone numbers.

64 Follow Up Every Contact With a Note, Letter ▬ ▬ ▬

Follow-up is crucial in the fundraising profession.

Whether as a cultivation tool or to provide additional information or to confirm something, make a point to follow up all face-to-face visits with a handwritten note or letter.

And while e-mails can serve as a follow-up method, traditional mail will have a greater impact.

Here are three examples of letter formats you could present to your volunteers.

John:

I just wanted to thank you for taking a few minutes to meet with me and learn more about our programs and services.

I also appreciated the opportunity to learn more about your company and its products.

I'll get back to you in the next couple of weeks to follow up on my invitation to support this year's effort.

Sincerely,

Jim Everly

Dear Mary:

Shortly after we met the other day, I came across the enclosed article about restoring vintage furniture. With your love of antiques, I thought you might find it to be of interest, so I am sending it to you.

It was great seeing you again. Thanks for all you continue to do for Heartland and those we serve.

Randi Harbor

Kestle Academy

November 12, 2008

Mrs. Jane Sandvig
8 Maple Hill Road
Sanger Springs, OH

Dear Mrs. Sandvig:

Thank you for allowing me to meet with you this week to review the planned gift options available. I hope you found it useful to discuss them in some detail and that I was able to resolve your questions.

As we both agreed, the charitable gift annuity appears to be the logical choice based on the rate of return and tax benefits you would derive. At your suggestion, I will contact you again in about 30 days to arrange another appointment to address any further questions and proceed.

I know I speak for our entire school in expressing our gratitude for the generous gift you are anticipating. Your generosity will positively impact many lives for generations to come.

And thanks again for the strawberry jam! It was delicious!

Sincerely,

Ann Jung
Director of Development

---

65 Conflict Resolution Tip ▬ ▬ ▬

■ If a member criticizes you for a particular action or response to a situation, ask how he/she would have handled the matter under similar circumstances. This will help to both disengage a potential confrontation and get at a solution.

66 Website Idea ▬ ▬ ▬

Are you tailoring your website to the needs and interests of your volunteers?

Increasing numbers of nonprofit organizations — Wellesley College, Wellesley, MA (www.wellesley.edu/Resources/volunteer/index.html) — are including a volunteer tools page on their websites that volunteers can turn to for information and support.

Article Designation Key: Donors ▬▬▬   Members ▬▬▬   Volunteers ▬▬▬

67 E-mail Communications Appeal to Members ▪ ▪

E-mail can open doors with members.

At Habitat for Humanity-La Crosse Area (La Crosse, WI), officials began e-mailing a member newsletter after receiving numerous requests to do so.

Executive Director Cori Skolaski says the response was immediate when they included a paragraph in the organization's quarterly hard-copy newsletter inviting readers to go paperless by visiting the website and signing up for e-mail mailings.

Some 500 members are currently on the e-mail list, and Skolaski says the organization accomplishes electronic mailings on the cheap: Member names are in an Access database and officials use Microsoft Outlook to send e-mails.

What's the main benefit of using e-mail? "Increased communication with our members," Skolaski says. "We are now able to contact people about things that aren't economically feasible by mail."

For instance, she says, sending 5,000 invitations wouldn't be possible with a limited budget. Now, with the e-mail invitation option, it's easy to invite members on the e-mail list to ground breakings, home dedication ceremonies and other special events. Even if people are unable to attend, the invitation is excellent public relations, she says.

They also use e-mail for informational purposes, including its response to natural disasters like Hurricane Katrina. The organization made it clear from the start that e-mail addresses wouldn't be used to solicit donations.

All internal communication is conducted by e-mail as is day-to-day communication with the Habitat board of directors, committees and volunteers.

One drawback to using Outlook, Skolaski says, is the limited number of people that can be e-mailed at one time. The organization sends several batches, and staff manually updates e-mail addresses in both Access and Outlook.

Acknowledging that software exists to make e-mailing groups easier, she says they'll continue with their method as long as it is convenient to do so.

Source: Cori Skolaski, Executive Director, Habitat for Humanity-La Crosse Area, La Crosse, WI. Phone (608) 785-2373. E-mail: cori@habitatlacrosse.org

68 Communicate With Teens In Language They Understand ▪

For persons who do not fall into the age range of 13 to 19, teenagers may seem like they come from a different planet. Communicating with teens as a volunteer manager can seem daunting as you wonder if your message is having an impact.

To help guarantee your important information gets to your young volunteers, speak in their language. Use one or all of these teen-friendly techniques to get your message across:

✓ **Text messaging.** Send mass text messaging updates about your volunteer program to all volunteers with cell phones. Text-savvy teens will appreciate your efforts to communicate at their preferred level. Check with your cell phone provider to ensure you have an unlimited texting plan to prevent additional costs.

✓ **Facebook.** Set up a Facebook page at www.facebook. com specifically for your teen volunteers. Use this free online social network to post volunteer-relevant topics, schedules and events. Volunteers who sign up as fans of the page will receive automatic notification when content is updated.

✓ **Internet presence.** Create a Web page specifically geared to teen volunteers. Add a page to your current website that makes announcements and includes updates for your teen volunteers, along with volunteer activities, group schedules and kudos for teens who deserve a pat on the back.

69 Listening Skills Tip ▪ ▪ ▪

Because listening speed is faster than speaking speed, try to consciously focus on the words someone is saying as well as their body language. Don't be shy about asking for details once the individual has completed his/her remarks.

70 Set Up Phone Hotline To Contact Mass of Volunteers at Once ▪

The problem: You need to get important information out to all your volunteers — fast.

One solution: Send an e-mail to all volunteers in your address book.

One glitch: Not all volunteers have e-mail, or check it daily, if they do.

Because of this dilemma, Sahily Picon, volunteer coordinator, Humane Society of Greater Miami (Miami, FL), created a volunteer hotline. Now, volunteers call a telephone number to hear an updated list of special events for which they are needed. Those interested in volunteering leave a message, and Picon gets back to them.

The hotline works just like an answering machine message, allowing volunteers to get updates without requiring Picon or others to make hundreds of phone calls.

Source: Sahily Picon, Volunteer Coordinator, Humane Society of Greater Miami, North Miami Beach, FL. Phone (305) 749-1821. E-mail: sahily@humanesocietymiami.org

71 Offer Cost-effective, Accessible Membership Kits Online ▬

The Ottawa Valley Tourist Association (OVTA) of Pembroke, Ontario, Canada, offers a simple and cost-effective approach toward membership kits. Instead of mailing expensive hard copies of kits and incurring rising postage and printing costs, this membership organization offers a downloadable membership kit at its website.

The OVTA has more than 225 members, and officials continue to build on that with the accessible membership kit, which averages 97 downloads each month.

The kit consists of three PDFs: a membership benefits form (at right), as well as a membership application and advertising rate card.

The kit also alerts the OVTA to new businesses coming to the region and those in the planning stages, says Nicole Wilson, communications coordinator.

"It has become an extremely popular way to attract members," Wilson says. "With less paper and postage, it saves money while helping the environment."

View the membership kit at www.ottawavalley.org.

Source: Nicole Wilson, Communications Coordinator, Ottawa Valley Tourist Association, Pembroke, Ontario, Canada. Phone (800) 757-6580. E-mail: NWilson@countyofrenfrew.on.ca

Content not available in this edition

72 Turn Criticism Into Constructive Feedback ▬

Carolyn B. Thompson, president, Training Systems Inc. (Frankfort, IL), prefers the term feedback over criticism. Criticism conveys a negative, while feedback encompasses both positive and negative comments. Constructive feedback provides information that can help solve the problem.

Pinpoint the specific issue you want to address. For example, instead of saying, "I heard you haven't been coming in on time," be more specific: "One of your clients called to say that you've been coming in at 9:30, rather than 9 a.m." The second statement is based on fact, versus opinion. The factual approach conveys a calm demeanor. "If you begin with emotion or opinion, the volunteer might stop listening before you reach an explanation," says Thompson.

Always give negative feedback in private, she cautions. Provide positive feedback in private as well, unless you're certain the volunteer would appreciate public recognition.

Source: Carolyn B. Thompson, President, Training Systems Inc., Great Training for Great Employees, Frankfort, IL. Phone (815) 469-1162. E-mail: cbt@trainingsys.com

Content not available in this edition

Article Designation Key:	Donors ▬	Members ▬	Volunteers ▬

74 Donor Impact Reports Help Illustrate How Gifts Make a Positive Difference ▪

Donor relations staff at The University of Kansas Hospital (Kansas City, KS) create donor impact reports to communicate to donors how their gift has made a positive difference to the area or program to which it was designated.

"Impact reports communicate our stewardship of their gift and keep donors engaged in future developments of the institution," says Andrea Villasi, program coordinator of donor relations for hospital fund development. "Frequent, personalized communication with your donors demonstrates the institution's and the fundraiser's responsibility to the donor. Communications like these strengthen the relationship with the donor."

Reports are customized to fit the size and scope of the gift and donor's personality, Villasi says. They are usually two to three pages long and include financial information, how the gift was used and plans for the remainder of the gift.

"Since our institution is a hospital, we also include stories about how our physicians, nurses and other staff have touched patients' lives," she says. "Adding color, photos and different fonts make the reports interesting and enticing to the donor."

While any level donor may receive a report, Villasi says because the documents are so personal and detailed, they are usually reserved for major donors, those under cultivation or with whom the hospital has a special relationship.

Reports are generally sent one year after a gift is made, she says. "Any less than that and we might not have enough data to warrant a comprehensive report. Any more than 18 months might make a statement to the donor that we have forgotten about them, or that we aren't utilizing their gift as expected."

The number of reports donors receive depends on their relationship with the hospital, gift lifespan and if donor has capacity or intention to give again. Many donors receive an impact report once a year until the fund is depleted or purpose

of the gift has been fulfilled.

For organizations considering using donor impact reports as a stewardship tool, Villasi offers this advice:

"Know your donors and customize their reports to fit their personalities. If they are business savvy and are driven to give as an investment in their community, for example, the report should focus more on the financial outcomes of their gift. If the donor was compelled to give because

of an emotional experience, touching stories of how their gift has helped others will mean more to them than the amount of investment income that their gift has accrued in the last year."

Source: Andrea Villasi, Program Coordinator, Donor Relations, Hospital Fund Development, The University of Kansas Hospital, Westwood, KS. Phone (913) 588-1433. E-mail: avillasi@kumc.edu

This sample donor impact report illustrates how donor relations staff at The University of Kansas Hospital (Kansas City, KS) personalize information to specific donors.

Content not available in this edition

75 Use Your Chapter Newsletter To Share Successes ▬ ▬ ▬

If you have several volunteer chapters in place throughout your region, state or nation, a regularly distributed newsletter — directed to all chapters — can be a valuable tool to spur chapters toward achievement. Featuring one chapter's recent accomplishments, for instance, may motivate members of other chapters to duplicate their efforts.

To get the most from sharing chapter achievements with other chapters, implement these ideas:

- To help identify individual chapter accomplishments — for future newsletter issues — include a form in your chapter newsletter for readers to complete and return to your office.

- When you list individual chapter accomplishments in your newsletter, be sure to include a contact name, phone number and e-mail address so readers can easily make a connection if they want more details on how to duplicate the idea.

- Include a regular chapter success story of the month in each newsletter issue.

- As a way to encourage friendly competition among chapters, begin a chapter accomplishment article with a headline: Can You Top This? Then invite readers to send in their own success stories for a future newsletter issue.

77 Ask the 'Passion Question' ▬

Rather than telling your donors what fund to contribute to, ask the "passion question," suggests Lola Mauer, director of annual giving, University of South Carolina (Columbia, SC).

Ask your donors: "What is an area or program that you can support that would really mean a lot to you?"

Help donors identify their passions and connect those passions to your cause, and the gifts will follow.

Source: Lola Mauer, Director of Annual Giving, University of South Carolina, Columbia, SC. Phone (803) 777-4092.
E-mail: lmauer@sc.edu

78 Be Accessible After Hours ▬

Any phone call by a volunteer (or potential volunteer) to a closed office is almost a warning to the caller: "Call me at my convenience, not yours."

During evenings and weekends have an answering machine turned on to direct those who may wish to assist your efforts or need help with an assigned project. Including your home or cell phone number and even an e-mail address shows you are accessible even when the office is closed.

76 Reach Professional Members With Roundtable Discussions ▬

Started as a group of female wine industry professionals teaming up to share ideas, Women for WineSense (Napa, CA) has grown into a wine education and networking organization that supports wine industry professionals as well as wine enthusiasts.

With 715 members in 12 chapters nationwide, Women for WineSense has become a strongly affiliated group. Membership levels and annual dues include corporate ($5,000), professional ($80), wine aficionado ($40) and student ($25). The largest membership levels are wine aficionado and professional, with most professional members residing in California's Sonoma and Napa regions, where winemaking is a predominant industry.

The Napa/Sonoma chapter is growing rapidly, in part because the chapter has beefed up what it offers professional members, says Karen Jess-Lindsley, president. For instance, the chapter has developed roundtable discussions where professional members can meet with industry peers to problem solve. Guidelines on conducting roundtable discussions to draw more professional members include:

❑ Limiting roundtable numbers to around 12 and including a diverse group (e.g., members from multinational corporations to boutique wineries) to diversify conversations.

❑ Selecting a roundtable head knowledgeable in the topic to set up and facilitate the meetings as well as notify participating members of the meeting.

❑ Communicating outcomes only to roundtable participants and members. This is a benefit of membership and retains confidentiality of the roundtable participants.

❑ Continuing roundtable discussions indefinitely. Offering monthly and bi-monthly discussions allows members to gather frequently and discuss timely issues.

"What we're finding is that there is a real need to connect with peers ... in a nonthreatening, noncompetitive way," the president says. "Roundtable discussions provide a forum for members to have these discussions and facilitate professional and career growth."

Source: Karen Jess-Lindsley, President, Women for WineSense, Napa, CA. Phone (800) 204-1616.
E-mail: Karen@lindsleyconsulting.com

79 E-mail Advice ▬

When putting out an e-mail call for help, send individual e-mails rather than a mass e-mail. If people see a request went to many others, they may feel less obligated to step forward and lend a hand.

80 Online Survey Questionnaires — Getting Member Feedback ▪

The Fox Cities Chamber of Commerce (Appleton, WI) has introduced a new opportunity to its members to receive feedback. In December 2008, the chamber initiated an online survey that can be completed anonymously by members to provide unabashed feedback to the chamber.

The member satisfaction survey takes up little time for the survey taker while providing the chamber a wealth of information on how it is doing in the eyes of its members.

"The member satisfaction survey asks all members to rate such things as benefits offered through the chamber, programs to grow the economy, community development involvement, membership events and communications material," says Pamela Hull, vice president-membership & operations. "It is important to take measure of what our membership is all about."

The online survey asks 10 pointed questions, including:

1. How would you assess the value you derive from chamber membership?
2. Which chamber affinity programs do you use?
3. How would you rate the value of the benefits listed above?
4. How would you rate membership events?
5. How would you rate the events and/or programs for economic development and legislative action?
6. How would you rate chamber communications?
7. How would you rate the responsiveness and professionalism of the chamber staff?
8. How would you assess the overall effectiveness of the chamber as an organization?
9. What input can you provide regarding priorities the chamber should address?
10. Is there anything the chamber can do to better serve your firm?

Response options range from excellent to poor and some questions include the rating of a variety of subcategories such as listing specific events offered by the chamber that can be rated under question No. 4.

Chamber staff calls on members during their Project Thank-You campaign and asks that members complete the survey. To date, 6 percent of the chamber's 1,700 members have completed the survey. To bring up that response rate, Hull and her staff will ask members once more to respond to the survey.

After compiling the survey results, Hull will then discuss the results with the board and staff any adjustments needed to better the chamber.

Source: Pamela Hull, Vice President-Membership & Operations, Fox Cities Chamber of Commerce, Appleton, WI. E-mail: phull@foxcitieschamber.com

81 Dos and Don'ts for Sharing Your Story With Donors ▪

When it comes to engaging persons in your cause and turning them into donors, telling them your story is crucial.

Sharing your story through feature articles in newsletters, in the news media, on your website, in public presentations, in one-on-one solicitations and other means is a cornerstone of a strong donor base.

Joseph Barbato, president, Barbato Associates (Alexandria, VA), offers some dos and don'ts for sharing your story when working with potential donors.

"A nonprofit should tell a compelling story that speaks directly to the interests of the donor," Barbato says. "A story should stress the tremendous difference the nonprofit is making in its field, which is one about which the donor is excited."

When communicating this message to potential donors, he says, there are four areas to avoid:

1. Negativity.
2. Overselling.
3. Taking the donor for granted.
4. Talking about how much better your nonprofit is than the other guys.

"The biggest challenge is getting the story just right," Barbato says. "You want to push all the right buttons and convey the story in the simplest and most memorable way. You must know your own organization and its strengths. What is it about your group that appeals to major gift donors? Why do they care? Study yourself, know yourself and act on the power of that self-understanding."

To accomplish this, Barbato offers the following tips:

❑ Hone your message.

❑ Keep it simple.

❑ Use telling anecdotes.

❑ Convey the emotion that goes with making a difference in people's lives.

❑ Make clear the wonderful opportunity the donor has to help advance your work and improve the lives of those your organization serves.

Source: Joseph Barbato, President, Barbato Associates, Alexandria, VA. Phone (703) 379-5441. E-mail: jb@barbatoassociates.com

82 Show Donors the Money (and Where It Goes) ▮

Anything you can do to show donors how their gifts make a difference will increase donors' confidence and make them more likely to give in the future.

Colleen Townsley Brinkmann, chief marketing officer, North Texas Food Bank (Dallas, TX), says a website illustration helps show donors where their food and financial donations go.

Visitors to the organization's website (www.ntfb.org) simply click on "Donate," then "Food" to find the link to the graphic chart, "Follow Your Donation."

Shown below, the graphic illustrates how food donations benefit 917 feeding and education programs in a 13-county area.

The page also helps educate donors and others about the work of the food pantry, which Townsley Brinkmann says is paramount: "We were having trouble getting people to understand we're not a cozy, little food pantry — we're a distribution agency. (And) by helping us you are helping tens of thousands of people."

The page averages 754 hits per month.

Source: Colleen Townsley Brinkmann, Chief Marketing Officer; Mark Armstrong, Senior Manager-Internet and New Media, North Texas Food Bank, Dallas, TX. Phone (214) 347-9594.

Website Offers Giving Tools

Visitors to the North Texas Food Bank (Dallas, TX) website find several tools to encourage gifts. For example, starting at the home page (www.ntfb.org), visitors can:

Learn how to start an actual or virtual canned food drive — Click "Donate," "Food," and select "Conduct a Canned or Virtual Food Drive" in pop-up menu to register and receive tips for gathering food or cash gifts.

See inside the food bank — Select "About Us" and "Virtual Tour."

Share the passion — Click "Media Room" and "Video Features" for online videos explaining food bank programs and how they help combat hunger in North Texas.

This online illustration shows North Texas Food Bank donors how their gifts help others.

83 Blogging Tip ▮ ▮ ▮

Associations and nonprofits are increasingly turning to blogs — an online journal typically updated daily — as a way to keep members up to date on issues, accomplishments and events.

If you maintain a member blog, make a point to include links throughout your copy that will provide additional insight or resources related to featured topics.

These organizations offer examples of links placed within their blogs:

American Library Association
http://blogs.ala.org/memberblog.php

Walker Art Center (Minneapolis, MN)
http://blogs.walkerart.org/newmedia

Greenpeace
http://members.greenpeace.org/blog/staff_oceans

Content not available in this edition

84 How to Overcome the Unresponsive Prospect ▮

You've just met a new major gift prospect, but the conversation appears to be going nowhere. The individual is hardly saying a word. Now what?

When dealing with unresponsive personalities:

1. Ask open-ended questions that require more than a "yes" or "no" response.

2. Once you ask a question, remain silent. Longer pauses force the person to respond.

3. Ask questions requiring the person to address a topic that interests him/her.

85 Trusted Private Social Networks Provide Secure Option for Members ▬

Private Social Networking Also Benefits Organizations

Loughlin says a member organization that utilizes private social networks will benefit in several ways:

- The network creates a clear and compelling value for the organization's brand. When members are able to connect, interact and share knowledge freely within the community, they associate that positive experience with the organization.

- Organizations can market more effectively to members by using online tools to reach members with personalized, relevant communications. Tapping into the personal profiles maintained by members also provides valuable insights on the community.

- Members have the tools necessary to help one another, which translates into real value for them — and for membership in the organization.

- Increases member retention. Members find value in extending their physical relationships into the online environment. They can become more easily involved in a variety of programs, forums and activities — both online and off.

- Members invite friends and colleagues to join the community. These free word-of-mouth referrals drive down new member acquisition costs.

Trusted Social Networks

Following is a sampling of Affinity Circles customers:

- ✓ Baylor University
- ✓ Delta Sigma Pi
- ✓ Johns Hopkins University
- ✓ University of Missouri
- ✓ Wartburg College
- ✓ University of Florida
- ✓ Asia America MultiTechnology Association

Looking for new ways to create networking opportunities for your members? Consider a private social network, such as Affinity Circles (Mountain View, CA).

Established in 2002, Affinity Circles was a trusted and secure community created by Stanford University students for both students and alumni who wanted to stay in contact with friends and colleagues. In 2003, the private social networking application was marketed to fellow alumni associations and organizations that could benefit from a member-based online community. Now more than 100 organizations use Affinity Circles platform for social networking.

Steve Loughlin, president and chief executive officer, explains the logistics of a private social network:

What are private social networks?

"A private social network is a secure online community that is accessible only to members of an alumni or professional organization that hosts it. Within this exclusive community, friends connect with friends, search for jobs, share expert knowledge, join professional groups, and share photos and blogs, all with the comfort of knowing their personal and professional communications are taking place within a secure setting they can trust."

How can a private online community help like-minded members?

"The trusted nature of a private community creates a unique environment for professional interactions. Because everyone is authenticated prior to entry, and all members share the same affinity, there is an increased sense of trust and rapport that encourages connections and an above-average willingness to help fellow community members. In addition, members have the tools necessary to easily target others for insight, expertise, job leads or referrals and more. It's also easy to form groups or discussion topics based on interests, which in turn promotes knowledge sharing and builds stronger relationships within the community."

How to Host A Private Social Network

Louglin says there are four steps involved in launching a private social networking community through Affinity Circles:

1. Sign a contractual agreement with Affinity Circles.

2. Provide graphics to Affinity Circles that brand the space for your community (e.g., a logo, your organization's name, etc.)

3. Upload your membership database records. This will enable community members to identify people by location, profession and/or name from day one of the community's launch, unlike other networking sites.

4. Affinity Circles launches the community.

How do private social networks work?

"To gain entry, each member must be authenticated. Once inside, members are free to connect with one another, collaborate and share knowledge among themselves through events, forums, blog feeds, photo sharing. In addition, members can take advantage of inCircle Jobs, an online recruiting service that allows employers to target job postings directly to the private online communities of alumni and professional organizations."

For more information on private social networks, visit www.affinitycircles.com.

Source: Steve Loughlin, President and Chief Executive Officer, Affinity Circles, Mountain View, CA. Phone (650) 810-1500. E-mail: sloughlin@affinitycircles.com

Article Designation Key: Donors ▬▬   Members ▬▬   Volunteers ▬▬

86 Educate Donors, Community Through Newspaper Column

Enid Ablowitz, vice president for strategic philanthropy, University of Colorado Foundation (Boulder, CO), writes a monthly column on philanthropy for her local newspaper, the Daily Camera.

"I think of my column as a community service," Ablowitz says. "I don't think of it as a marketing tool."

The editor asked her to write regularly after she penned a guest opinion in support of a local foundation's innovative idea to create an endowment to support nonprofits. In the eight years since, she has written on topics such as endowments, year-end giving, charitable gift annuities, and most recently, elevator speeches.

Columns, around 750 words long, include her byline and titles as associate director of the University of Colorado's Coleman Institute for Cognitive Disabilities and vice president for strategic philanthropy at the CU Foundation.

"The topic of philanthropy has become a regular feature," Ablowitz says.

"People read my column because they know I will give them information and advice without expecting anything in return," she says. "I believe that if people are armed with the knowledge about the strategies and mechanisms for giving, they will be more inclined to give — and they derive more satisfaction from it."

She offers advice for development professionals considering writing a regular column on philanthropy:

- Do so only if your motive is educational. Treat readers with respect.

- Check your facts to ensure everything you write is accurate.

- Use a conversational style.

- Make sure gift planning articles offer information on charitable intent. Charitable giving vehicles are means to provide a gift; tax and other financial benefits should be secondary.

- When addressing specific giving techniques, always recommend that readers consult with their advisor or attorney before making a gift.

- Most of all, celebrate donors and connect gifts with the impact they have.

Source: Enid M. Ablowitz, Vice President for Strategic Philanthropy, University of Colorado Foundation, Boulder, CO. E-mail: enid.ablowitz@cufund.org

87 Newsletter Profiles Members ■ ■ ■

Jeff Carter, newsletter editor, The Society for Technical Communication, Snake River Chapter (Boise, ID), includes a member profile in each monthly issue.

"We ask new members if they would answer a series of questions about their education and work backgrounds, job, hobbies and interests," says Carter.

The articles make new members feel welcome, the editor says. "We have a global organization, but local chapters across the world are where the organization gets its strength. We find that new members really like to participate in the profile because it allows them to say hello to their local chapter."

Member profiles also make the newsletter more personal, says Carter: "Our members are as interested in people as they are in tools and technologies, so having a profile lets everyone learn a little about a new member of their own community." Read a profile at: www.stc-src.org/newsletter/1004/profile.htm

Source: Jeff Carter, Editor, Society for Technical Communication, Snake River Chapter, Boise, ID. Phone (208) 321-4412. E-mail: catchtrout@excite.com

88 Tips for Communicating With Members ■ ■ ■

Simple yet effective tools can make communicating with volunteers much easier.

Tara Fitzgerald, national director of volunteer programs, PKD Foundation (Kansas City, MO), explains three steps her organization took in the last year to communicate more efficiently with volunteers nationwide:

1. Posting a page on the national website accessible only by volunteers that features handbooks, forms and an electronic submission system where they can request various pre-event forms and materials or submit a website update.

2. Creating a monthly volunteer newsletter, Coordinator Connection, where the national office shares important information with volunteers;

3. Rather than having volunteers who may be organizing an event use personal e-mail addresses, setting up specialized e-mails such as iowachapter@pkdcure.org or specialevent@pkdcure.org. Doing so, Fitzgerald says, helps protect established groups and activities from turnover by providing a consistent contact point.

Source: Tara Fitzgerald, National Director of Volunteer Programs, PKD Foundation, Kansas City, MO. Phone (816) 931-2600. E-mail: taraf@pkdcure.org. Website: www.pkdcure.org

| Article Designation Key: | Donors ▨ | Members ▨ | Volunteers ▨ |

89 Prepare to Overcome Membership Objections ■

You've taken all the right initial first steps with that potential new member, including detailing membership benefits, going on a tour of your facility and providing written materials about your organization.

So why isn't the person completing the membership application? What are the person's objections, and how should you best respond to them to lead the person to join your organization?

Using a method called Feel, Felt, Found, you'll more easily win over someone who may be riding the fence to membership. Here are three examples of how to overcome common objections to membership using the method:

Objection: I don't have the time to participate in a membership organization.

Response: I understand how you feel — everyone is so busy these days. When I became a member "x" years ago, I too felt I was too busy to commit to membership. What I've found is I've been able to adjust my level of participation to accommodate my schedule. And the benefits make membership well worth the time!

Objection: I don't think I'll get much out of a membership.

Response: I understand where you're coming from, but I can tell you that since I've joined, I've felt more focused on my goals and have benefited both personally and professionally through my membership. I'm certain you'll find the same benefits.

Objection: I can't afford membership fees.

Response: When I joined, it felt like a lot of money at first, too. What I've found is that the benefits (cite several exceptional ones) far outweigh cost of membership. Membership has also increased my networking ability in the area, which has greatly improved my bottom line as well. The membership is benefiting my career. (Cite payment methods and options, if available).

This Feel, Felt, Found technique shows potential members you empathize with their concerns and you're willing to help them find solutions. Remaining positive and showing concern while you help persons interested in membership will leave a positive impression that will hopefully lead to their signing on as members.

90 Gear Volunteer Presentations to the Age of Your Audience ■

Hone training presentations to participants' age to help ensure they learn all they need from the sessions. Here are factors to consider based on the age of your volunteers:

❑ **Mature Adults** — Revise materials and presentation to accommodate persons with vision or hearing problems. Create handouts with larger type, asking attendees if they would like such materials and offering regular handouts to others. Speak slowly and clearly. When adjusting your speaking volume, ask participants at the outset whether the volume of your voice is easy to hear and then adjust accordingly.

❑ **Youth** — Keep presentation pace lively to engage this group. Add music and keep interaction and exchanges animated. Use visual aids with concise bullet points and captivating graphics. Ask for ideas on how they can serve to gain ownership.

❑ **Middle Age** — This group is extraordinarily busy with life's demands, from career to children to aging parents. Make the presentation concise, clear and offer handouts to review at home. Include contact information — especially an e-mail address — so they can contact you for details or clarifications after the training.

91 Say No Nicely to Avoid Turning Volunteers Away ■

Believe it or not, some volunteer roles are so popular that organizations run out of openings. Nice problem to have, right?

When you have more than enough volunteers on board for a specific event or task, how do you gracefully tell people "thanks but no thanks" without turning them off from future volunteer opportunities with your cause?

Here are two tips for doing so:

❑ **First off, always be honest.** If the reason you have to

say no is because you have too many volunteers for one specific role or task, say so. Frame it in positive terms, such as, "We are so fortunate that so many people want to help. We've had an overwhelming response. We just can't accept any more volunteers right now."

❑ **Next, direct them to another appropriate role** and offer to keep their contact information on file in case circumstances should change.

92 Consider Webcam to Illustrate, Celebrate Building Process ▪

Do you have a major building project under way or on the horizon? Engage donors and potential donors in this exciting process to keep them involved and aware of the value of their support.

A webcam is helping capture the ongoing construction of the Bob and Shirley Hunter Welcome Center at Abilene Christian University (Abilene, TX).

"The webcam is a unique opportunity for us to connect donors to the project as well as those who have an interest in keeping up with developments on campus," says John Tyson, director of development. "It helps our friends and donors keep up with their investment and be reminded of how their funds are being used."

Before construction began, staff mounted a webcam to the university's campus bell tower and began shooting images of the construction site.

The webcam takes eight pictures per minute. Images are stored on a server and then uploaded to the university's website where visitors can click on a still image of the construction to view the live webcam (www.acu.edu/aboutacu/map_acu/webcam.html).

Images on the website are refreshed every 60 seconds.

Kevin Watson, who oversees construction projects on campus, says the webcam stayed up for the duration of the project.

With construction complete, the images were edited into a high-speed video showing the building, from ground breaking to finish, in about three minutes — a useful resource when talking with donors and potential donors.

The 57,000-square-foot facility is home to admissions, alumni relations, The ACU Foundation, the Center for Building Community and Career Center.

Sources: John Tyson, Director of Development; Kevin Watson, Administrative Services; Abilene Christian University, Abilene, TX. Phone (325) 674-2659 (Tyson) or (325) 674-2363 (Watson). E-mail: tysonj@acu.edu or watsonk@acu.edu

---

How a Webcam Works

The webcam capturing the construction of the Bob and Shirley Hunter Welcome Center at Abilene Christian University (ACU) of Abilene, TX is wired into the campus network, says Arthur Brant, director of networking services. The webcam works like a still camera, automatically taking and saving eight pictures a minute.

"The camera has Web server software that allows it to take and store pictures, which a second intermediate server can grab and store," says Brant. "The pictures on the university's website (www.acu.edu/aboutacu/map_acu/webcam.html), taken from the intermediate server, are refreshed every 60 seconds."

The webcam can be set to take as many as 30 pictures a second (full-motion video) to eight pictures a minute.

"We chose to go with a lower per-minute capture so as to not overwhelm our servers," he says. "We began taking pictures in December 2007 and are expecting 12 months of construction. At eight pictures a minute, we are taking 11,520 pictures in a given day and 4.2 million pictures by the end of the construction period. That many pictures can take up a lot of storage space."

Brant says they are storing all the pictures from the webcam so that they can create a stop-motion video encapturing the entire project, start to finish.

Webcams cost $800 to $1,000 depending on the quality of the images captured, says Brant. ACU's mid-quality camera cost about $1,000, plus the cost of a wide-view lens.

"For our purposes we wanted a middle-of-the-road camera," says Brant. "We aren't trying to do full-motion videos. We were more interested in giving people the online experience of a webcam."

Source: Arthur Brant, Director of Networking Services, Abilene Christian University, Abilene, TX. Phone (325) 674-2930. E-mail: branta@acu.edu

---

93 Committee Liaisons Keep Communication Flowing ▪

If your organization has numerous volunteer committees involved with several different projects/programs, consider appointing one member of each committee as a liaison. Then meet with all liaisons as a group on a weekly or monthly basis to get updated on their committees' work. This way, you not only have a better understanding of each group's work, all committee reps also have a common knowledge about what the others are doing as well.

94 Volunteer Bulletin Boards Help to Recognize, Recruit ▪

Create a volunteer bulletin board in a high traffic area of your facility. Use it to:

✓ Post photos of new volunteers in action.

✓ List volunteer accomplishments.

✓ Include a volunteer photo and profile weekly (or monthly).

✓ Include a wish list of needs that have yet to be met through volunteer assistance.

✓ Post a calendar of upcoming events.

95 Media Partnerships Enhance Member Communications ■

Partner with the media to boost your ability to communicate with members.

The Association for Career and Technical Education (ACTE) of Alexandria, VA, teamed up with U.S. News and World Report to provide a daily news e-mail, Career Tech Update.

"Overall, this partnership has helped keep our members informed about what's happening on a national level," says Pete Magnuson, senior director of programs and communications. "In today's news environment — where news is reported and updated minute by minute — if our members are not informed by their professional association, we are doing them a disservice."

Since September 2007, U.S. News has delivered the e-mail every weekday morning as a free benefit to members.

Magnuson says U.S. News staff initiated the partnership. "After we met with them, we decided that a daily news roundup would be exactly what our members needed," he says. "ACTE has the image of a trusted source within the career and technical education industry, and this partnership seemed to blend right into that image."

Information for the updates is culled from thousands of U.S. News sources, as well as from ACTE.

"This truly is a partnership designed to keep our members informed about what is happening in career and technical education," says Magnuson. In addition to news from traditional mainstream sources, "we regularly include updates from the association or run stories that come from some of our sources."

Before sending the news update to the full membership, ACTE staff tested it with one membership category and gathered feedback, which helped work out some delivery issues.

So far, ACTE has received "tremendously positive feedback," Magnuson says, "but we will continue to monitor this new service and make any necessary changes or enhancements."

Source: Pete Magnuson, Senior Director of Programs and Communications, Association for Career and Technical Education, Alexandria, VA. Phone (800) 826-9972. E-mail: pmagnuson@acteonline.org

96 Newsletters: Capturing Compelling Copy ■ ■ ■

Members of the Just Food Co-op (Northfield, MN) enjoy a monthly newsletter called The ComPost, which is chock-full of information on current store happenings as well as news about natural food topics.

Most of the writing is done by non-staff persons by invitation of co-op staff.

Each month, Joey Robison, marketing and member services manager, seeks out community leaders and experts to fill the pages of the newsletter. She has found this to be an excellent way to get expertise from community members and to engage members.

"Inviting non-staff members to write for our newsletter makes it a much more interesting read, because it broadens the topics we can include and provides different perspectives," Robison says. "It also builds the feeling of community that we work to create. Readers and writers alike get a sense that the success of our store is based on the participation of each of us — shoppers, member-owners, board members and employees — not just the staff."

Robison shares her tips for capturing compelling newsletter copy:

❏ **Brainstorm relevant topics with staff and members.** Staff have a feel for what members want to read. Ask members and readers to offer their ideas for topics that would be most useful to them.

❏ **Select an expert in the field you wish to cover.** Robison explains to the person she approaches that he/she was hand selected to write articles and that he/she can offer a great voice for the topic.

❏ **Contact the community member directly by phone or in person to obtain his/her commitment.** Using guest writers is the ideal way to ensure expertise on any given topic and allows your writer an elevated profile and exposure in the community.

❏ **Create a set deadline calendar.** The fifth of the month is Robison's deadline for submissions and she sticks to it. Offer your guest writer a soft deadline that is one or two weeks prior to your hard deadline to ensure a timely submission.

Source: Joey Robison, Marketing and Member Services Manager, Just Food Co-op, Northfield, MN. Phone (507) 650-0106. E-mail: joeyr@justfood.coop

Four Steps to Effective Newsletters

The newsletter for the Just Food Co-op (Northfield, MN) is a well-written, interesting read. To accomplish this, co-op staff:

1. Offer tightly written articles with a specific focus.

2. Ensure that every article serves an educational purpose, but is written in a friendly, conversational tone.

3. Add a calendar in the newsletter to draw readers and inform recipients of upcoming events.

4. Create an area specifically to highlight classes available through the co-op. (Staff ask class participants how they learned of the opportunity to gauge effectiveness of the newsletter calendar and notices.)

97 Personalized Message Makes for Direct Mail Appeal Success

An appeal with a simple tagline, "Then, Now and Again," has yielded the best results in direct mail campaign history for the Hebrew Academy of Tidewater/Strelitz Early Childhood Center (Virginia Beach, VA).

Eilene Rosenblum, director of development, says each piece of the direct mail appeal is a four-fold, 5 1/2 X 9-inch brochure featuring a school year photo of a donor juxtaposed with a present family photo (where the children are the current students).

A quote from the donor expressing gratitude for life lessons learned at the academy is featured under the family photo, with information on his/her subsequent education.

The brochure's next two pages feature text on the school's mission and need for financial support, mixed with photos of students who attend the K-6 and preschool division.

Mailed in three parts — August, December and April — the direct mail appeal was sent to 3,000 donors and prospective donors.

Unlike past years when donors who contributed after the first mailing were not sent additional mailings, Rosenblum says all 3,000 persons on the list received all three mailings, plus a thank-you note if they donated, so they could see the complete campaign.

This tactic — along with the use of former students at the center of the appeal's message — proved a winning com-bination, bringing in 500 gifts totaling more than $350,000. The average gift was $500 and the largest, $2,500.

"This approach yielded the best results for a direct mail appeal we have ever produced," says Rosenblum, pointing to the $50,000 increase in gifts over the prior year's annual campaign. "The personalized appeal resonated with recipients not only because they recognized themselves, but because they recognized their contemporaries. It also resonated with older people who saw their children or their children's children following in their footsteps."

Rosenblum says the mailing was such a success she is using it again for the upcoming year, featuring new participants and their families.

"The personalized apped resonated with recipients not only because they recognized themselves, but because they recognized their contemporaries."

Source: Eilene Rosenblum, Director of Development, Hebrew Academy of Tidewater/Strelitz Early Childhood Center, Virginia Beach, VA. Phone (757) 424-4327.
E-mail: Ehrosenblum@hebrewacademy.net

Juxtaposing a past class picture with the student today proved successful for a direct mail appeal for the Hebrew Academy of Tidewater/Strelitz Early Childhood Center (Virginia Beach, VA).

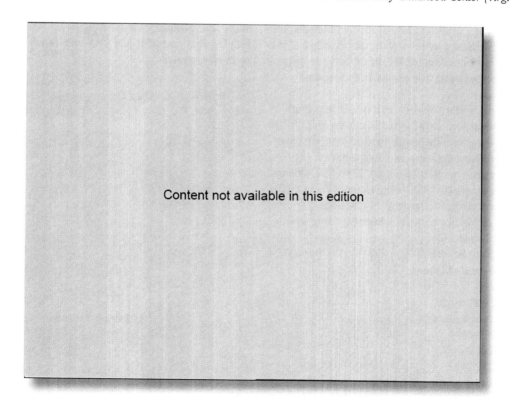

Content not available in this edition

98 Show Membership Value Through Dynamic Video ■■

Give prospective members a behind-the-scenes look at all the excitement happening at your organization with a video spotlighting major benefits and events.

You could structure the video as "A Day in the Life of XYZ Organization" and ask a couple members to allow a staff member armed with a video camera to follow them through committee meetings, networking events or a member field trip.

Have members speak directly to the camera and share their thoughts on the event as well as some lighthearted stories or fun memories relating to their membership.

Get some video and input from staff as well as they interact with members or prepare for the meeting or event.

Be sure to get written permission from each person you film, whether they are one of your members or one of your staff.

Post the video on your website and direct persons to the link in recruitment letters and e-mails to prospective members.

More detailed than a simple testimonial video, a video of this kind will provide prospective members with insight into how your organization treats members, what members experience, and how your services and programs may benefit them.

99 Tailor Brochures to Targeted Age Groups ■

Finding it difficult to appeal to different age groups in one direct mail appeal? Why not do what officials with Agnes Scott College (Decatur, GA) did with their annual fund mailings?

Agnes Scott's annual fund brochures, which won a CASE (Council for Advancement and Support of Education) award, were targeted to specific groups of alumnae.

"At an annual fund staff meeting, we were talking about how difficult it is to write a letter which appeals to all age groups," says Joanne Davis, director of annual fund. "We discussed how far apart in ages our alumnae are, from in their 90s to their early 20s, and wondered if there wasn't something different we could do to connect with them and catch their attention."

The brainstorming phase of the project involved gaining perspectives from several people — alumnae director (a 1968 alumna), creative services director, freelance designer, annual fund officer (a 2003 alumna), two associate annual fund directors and Davis.

"After much discussion, we decided it would be a good idea to divide and conquer," says Davis. "In other words, divide our constituency into groups by decades and do four brochures for alumnae and one for current parents and parents of alumnae." The groups were older alumnae ('25 to '59), alumnae ('60s to '79), alumnae ('80 to '92), young alumnae ('93 to '03) and current students' parents and parents of graduates.

Each mailer included a photo montage featuring an age-appropriate alumna with nostalgic photos from her era and the theme, "The Power of One — The Impact of Many."

"We thought they might pay more attention to a piece that contained few words but had pictures that would evoke nostalgia and make them understand every gift is important and every gift, large or small, makes a difference,"

says Davis. "We wanted something that would catch their attention immediately and make them think about the college and the part it played in their life."

> *"We wanted something that would catch their attention immediately and make them think about the college and the part it played in their life."*

The college got a lot of mileage out of the brochures' theme. An e-solicitation with music and some of the same photos was a big hit, says Davis, but unfortunately, they weren't able to track results. The brochures brought in about $30,000 that they were able to track.

The images on the front of the brochures were used to make four postcards for fund chairs to write thank-you notes. Final appeal postcards and year-end, thank-you postcards were also created.

Source: Joanne A. Davis, Director of Annual Fund, Office of Development, Agnes Scott College, Decatur, GA.
Phone (404) 471-5343. E-mail: jadavis@agnesscott.edu

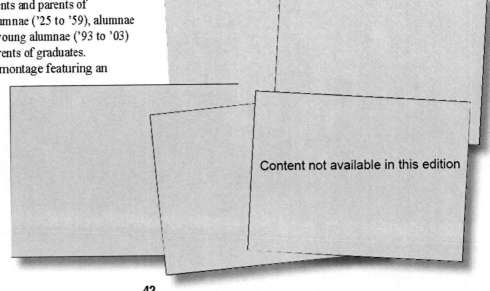

Content not available in this edition

Article Designation Key: Donors ■■■■   Members ■■■■   Volunteers ■■■■

100 Refine E-mails to Members to Reduce Opt-out Rates ▪

If a significant percentage of your members opt out of e-mail communications, take a closer look at how you're using this important communications method. Then brainstorm ways to make more worthwhile e-mail connections with members.

According to Wes Trochlil, president, Effective Database Management (Hamilton, VA), many organizations send members e-mails weekly, if not daily. This overabundance of e-communications could result in an increase of opt-outs as members ask to be removed from your e-mail recipient list.

Track your opt-out rates for two months, Trochlil suggests: "If the current opt-out rate is 0.5 percent and there is a jump to 5 percent, the organization may be experiencing an opt-out problem."

The No. 1 reason members opt out of e-mail communications? Irrelevancy, he says: "Members will say they're being inundated with messages from their member organization, but what they really mean is they're inundated with irrelevant information."

To curb that problem, Trochlil offers these suggestions:

- **Assess a member's behavior.** Organizations need to know and understand what is important to the member.

They need to ask: "What publications does he/she buy? What meetings does he/she attend? How long has he/she been a member? Which special interest groups does he/she belong to?"

> The No. 1 reason members opt out of e-mail lists? Irrelevancy.

- **Segment the opt-out message.** Instead of providing a generalized opt-out message, segment it so members can customize what they receive. For example, allow members to opt out of certain communications without saying no to all e-mails (e.g., opting out of certification announcements but not event announcements).

- **Personalize your e-mails.** "E-communications are expected to be personalized these days, otherwise the recipients think you are a rookie," he says. "Even though they know the message is being sent by a machine, it is received better by the member's subconscious if it is personally addressed to the intended recipient."

Source: Wes Trochlil, President, Effective Database Management, Hamilton, VA. Phone (540) 338-9404.
E-mail: wes@effectivedatabase.com

101 Gain Insight With Member Polls ▪

Encouraging members to vote in online polls is an easy and cost-effective way to get their opinions on a wide variety of subjects.

The Alumni Association of Barry University (Miami Shores, FL) began using online polls in the summer of 2008. Alumni relations staff change questions monthly, with roughly 500 to 1,000 members responding to each question.

Sean Kramer, assistant vice president, alumni relations, says he came up with the member poll idea as a way to make the alumni site more interactive. Currently, responses received by members are only used as anecdotal information and are not published. However, he says they will most likely publish poll responses in future issues of their e-news and alumni magazines.

Kramer shares a few examples of recent poll questions:

- What are your opinions of the new alumni association website?

- Have you attended an alumni association event in the past 6 months?

- How often do you utilize alumni association member benefits?

The university's information technology staff creates the online poll feature at no cost. The four-person alumni relations team comes up with the poll questions and IT staff update the poll each month with the new question. Aside from

including the poll feature on the alumni association website's home page, the polls are also mentioned in the university's e-news, which includes a link encouraging alumni to cast their vote.

When considering questions to include on an online poll, Kramer says, ask yourself:

- Is it information that will enhance our programs?

- Is it information that will benefit our members?

"Using these questions as a guideline should help organizations determine what questions to ask and when," says Kramer.

When designing a member poll feature, place it in a prominent section of your website so all of your members will notice it. If you are not sure whether to implement a new service or policy, a member poll is a great way to gain some insight into how your members will react to the change. You can also include questions about upcoming campaigns and special events to gauge member interest.

Include a link to your member polls in your e-mail and written correspondence with members to provide them with another reminder to share their thoughts.

Source: Sean Kramer, Assistant Vice-President, Alumni Relations, Barry University, Miami Shores, FL. Phone (305) 899-4013.
E-mail: SeKramer@mail.barry.edu

102   Communicate With Donors About 'Underwater' Endowments ▪

Keeping major donors in the communications loop — even when the news is less than positive — is an important part of donor relations.

In February 2009, staff with Kent State University (Kent, OH) sent letters to 410 endowment donors informing them how the economy had impacted their endowments.

The letters, each hand-signed by the executive director of the Kent State University Foundation, were created from a template and personalized for each donor to include the name of the donor's endowment fund and its market value as of Dec. 31, 2008, as well as how much it had decreased since July 1, 2008.

"The third paragraph of the letter was also personalized based on the wording of each agreement and whether or not the scholarship was underwater (market value is less than its historic dollar value) after the downturn in the economic market," says Scott McKinney, associate director of stewardship. "We did not ask them to allow us to invade the principal, but have allowed amendments to the endowments if requested."

Seven donors requested that university officials amend their agreements to allow invasion of the principal, McKinney says, and two donors have requested that the university amend their agreements to not allow invasion of the principal. Seven donors have made additional gifts to ensure that their scholarship is awarded next year.

"We have received many positive comments from our donors about this letter," McKinney notes. "They seemed to appreciate our transparency, even though the news was less than positive."

Source: Scott McKinney, Associate Director, Stewardship, Institutional Advancement, Kent State University, Kent, OH. Phone (330) 672-0347. E-mail: smckinne@kent.edu

Officials from Kent State University (Kent, OH) share the template for a personalized letter informing endowment donors how the economy has impacted their endowments.

Content not available in this edition

103 E-news and Hot Sheets Take Place of Lengthy Newsletter ▬ ▬ ▬

At the Denver International Airport (DIA) of Denver, CO, communications with volunteers is critically important.

But Corinne Christensen, administrator of DIA's hospitality ambassador program, found newsletters a cumbersome way to communicate with volunteers. So she created an electronic communications tool — Friday E-News bulletins — and one-page handouts — hot sheets — to give volunteers up-to-the-minute updates to help them succeed.

Christensen answers questions about these new forms of volunteer communication:

What information is included in Friday E-News and what's included in hot sheets? How do they differ?

"Friday E-News is longer and contains the extra kind of news and computer items available to more than 260 volunteers, some employees and administration.

"E-News contains airport news and information (press releases; airline changes; passenger boarding forecasts; airport services updates; airport concessions and business updates; airport business updates that affect volunteers; events that involve the airport); community and tourist information (conferences traveling through airport and their transportation information; events that include the airport); and volunteer program news and information (volunteer shift updates for week; information about other airport volunteer programs; holiday information that affect the program; computer tips and fun searches; birthdays; programs news; volunteer anecdotes and thank-you notes; important dates).

"The hot sheet (shown right) is one-page, double-sided and more condensed with less detail, available for each shift during the week at shift meetings. The hot sheet contains press releases or timely airport news; motivating information for volunteers; shift information; airport updates and weekly dates."

How much time do you save doing this versus creating a typical newsletter?

"I save around a week's worth of time by doing the E-News on Fridays. I can include shorter amounts of information rather than the typical newsletter articles, which had to be edited by public information officers of our public relations division; they trust me to be informative, spell-checked and succinct!"

Who receives these communications? Are they geared to volunteers?

"The E-News and the hot sheet are geared for the volunteers, but our customer service employees and security officers like to have them simply because the airport no longer has a weekly newspaper. I double-check everything to make sure it is public knowledge before I include that information in updates."

What are some specific tips you could share with other volunteer managers about creating these two publications?

✓ "Use the same format with each publication so your audience can check updated information at a glance.

✓ "Check your sources regularly to see where they are getting their information — I was once using a database that was waiting for my E-News to update the database — the information was going around in circles!

✓ "Add something personal in your news: a thank-you to a volunteer, a special anniversary date or something fun.

✓ "Include reminders that will help your great volunteers become wonderful volunteers.

✓ "Always include information that reminds volunteers of routine practices; such as, always take lost items to lost and found immediately, the website address of the volunteer program and the airport. I sometimes use these routine pieces as dividers between subjects, make them colorful and eye-catching."

Source: Corinne Christensen, Program Administrator, DIA Hospitality Ambassador Program, Denver, CO. Phone (303) 342-2243. E-mail: Corinne.Christensen@flydenver.com

Content not available in this edition

104 Sometimes a Letter of Introduction Is the Best Approach ▪

When making initial contact with a new major gift prospect, involving someone familiar with both your organization and the prospect is helpful, but not always possible.

In situations where you're the only individual capable of making an introduction, begin with a sincere letter that sets the stage for an appointment. If appropriate, mention that a mutual friend suggested you contact the prospect.

Remember these four additional points as you produce a letter of introduction:

1. To the degree possible, tailor your letter to the prospect's interests and personality.

2. Remember your primary objective: to have the opportunity to meet face to face.

3. Promise to limit your time to an hour or less.

4. Thank prospect in advance for agreeing to meet with you.

This sample letter illustrates how to approach a prospect with whom you have no prior connection.

September 20, 2009

Caring Hands
YOUTH SERVICES

Dr. and Mrs. Arthur Scott
4239 2nd Avenue North
Minneapolis, MN 55413

Dear Dr. and Mrs. Scott:

About two weeks ago your friends, Dr. and Mrs. Alan Feinstein, suggested I contact you simply to tell you about our agency and introduce you to some of what we are accomplishing throughout greater Minneapolis.

Caring Hands Youth Services was founded in 1978 to reach out to the youth of greater Minneapolis — ages 4 to 18 — as a means to nurture their God-given talents and support their families in preparing today's youth for tomorrow's challenges.

On average, Caring Hands works with some 15,000 youth on a yearly basis and has gained national recognition for some of our initiatives.

One of our more recent accomplishments, for instance, was to provide training for nearly 300 middle school children in web site development — a skill with increasing demand in this age of computer technology. And the resulting implications of this program are significant.

If you would be so kind as to give me just one hour of your time, I would like to tell you more about this and other programs and the difference they are making in the lives of our community's youth.

I will phone you within the next week to set a time and location convenient for both of you to meet. In the meantime, I thank you for your willingness to give me your attention.

Sincerely,

Megan A. Anderson
Director of Development

 ## 105 Boost Volunteer Contact by Tweeting With Twitter ▪

For many nonprofit organizations, social networking is the new norm when communicating with volunteers and staff.

Twitter (www.twitter.com) offers a new way to communicate with a number of individuals simultaneously using instant messaging via text messaging or online. In lieu of sending multiple messages to a variety of individuals, Twitter lets you reach a number of people with a single message.

Individual Twitter messages are referred to as tweets.

While Twitter allows you to send messages to many individuals at one time, it also allows you to gain feedback from this same group.

Use Twitter within your nonprofit to:

• Allow volunteers to view a window on your day.

• Take immediate polls from staff or volunteers to aid in decision making or implementing new ideas.

• Organize instant meetings called "Tweetups."

• Send positive messages about your nonprofit to a select group of volunteers.

• Send instant information to volunteers about changes in scheduling or new happenings at your nonprofit.

• Request that existing volunteers recruit a friend to volunteer.